Social responses to handicap

SOCIAL POLICY IN MODERN BRITAIN

General Editor: Jo Campling

HEALTH POLICY AND THE NATIONAL HEALTH SERVICES *Judy Allsop*
THE VOLUNTARY SECTOR IN BRITISH SOCIAL SERVICES *Maria Brenton*
HOUSING AND SOCIAL JUSTICE *Gill Burke*
EDUCATION AS SOCIAL POLICY *Janet Finch*
PENAL POLICY *Rod Morgan*
FOUNDATIONS OF THE WELFARE STATE *Pat Thane*
THE ELDERLY IN MODERN SOCIETY *Anthea Tinker*
SOCIAL RESPONSES TO HANDICAP *Eda Topliss*
THE PERSONAL SOCIAL SERVICES *Adrian Webb and Gerald Wistow*

SOCIAL RESPONSES TO HANDICAP

Eda Topliss

LONGMAN
London and New York

LONGMAN GROUP LIMITED
LONGMAN HOUSE
BURNT MILL, HARLOW, ESSEX, UK
Published in the United States of America
by Longman Inc., New York

First published 1982

British Library Cataloguing in Publication Data

Topliss, Eda
Social responses to handicap. — (Social policy in modern Britain)
1. Handicapped — Great Britain
I. Title II. Series
362.4'0941 HV1559.G6

ISBN 0-582-29538-6

Library of Congress Cataloging in Publication Data

Topliss, Eda.
Social responses to handicap.

(Social policy in modern Britain)
Bibliography: p.
Includes index.
1. Handicapped — Government policy — Great Britain.
2. Great Britain — Social policy. I. Title. II. Series.
HV1559.G6T653 362.4'0456'0941 81-18602
ISBN 0-582-29538-6 (pbk.) AACR2

Printed in Singapore by
The Print House (Pte) Ltd.

CONTENTS

EDITOR'S PREFACE

This series, written by practising teachers in universities and polytechnics, is produced for students who are required to study social policy and administration, either as social science undergraduates or on the various professional courses. The books provide studies focusing on essential topics in social policy and include new areas of discussion and research, to give students the opportunity to explore ideas and act as a basis of seminar work and further study. Each book combines an analysis of the selected theme, a critical narrative of the main developments and an assessment putting the topic into perspective as defined in the title. The supporting documents and comprehensive bibliography are an important aspect of the series.

Conventional footnotes are avoided and the following system of references is used. A superior numeral in the text refers the reader to the corresponding entry in the list of references at the end of each chapter. A select bibliography is found at the end of the book. A number in square brackets, preceded by 'doc', e.g. [doc 6, 8], refers the reader to the corresponding items in the section of documents which follows the main text.

Social Responses to Handicap sets out clearly and comprehensively the various provisions made by society for its handicapped population. Instead of merely listing the sequence of legislative enactments and administrative arrangements, the book gives greater coherence to the pattern of provision by relating it to different age groups of handicapped people – children, adults of working age, and the elderly.

In the second half of the book there is a penetrating and rather disturbing analysis of the factors affecting attitudes to disablement. Stigmatization of handicap is shown to be the inevitable outcome of the heavy emphasis which society puts on individual achievement, particularly in the occupational sphere. This emphasis is in turn shown to be an essential component of the modern, rationally organized, industrial society. In an illuminating final chapter the book relates the examination of the values which underly and inform the social reponse to handicap to a new explanatory theory of social policy in general.

Jo Campling

AUTHOR'S PREFACE

My concern with the problems of disablement springs from watching my only sister change from a sturdy childhood playmate to a twisted and heavily dependent cripple, disabled by a progressive disorder of the central nervous system. The reactions of society to her needs and to the needs of other disabled individuals were the starting point for this book, together with an urge to understand why those reactions are what they are. The indomitable courage of my sister, and of so many other disabled people I have met, inspired me to attempt this book, but I alone am responsible for any defects, errors or omissions.

Eda Topliss
July 1981

Part one
THE AGES OF DISABILITY

Chapter One
HANDICAP AND THE THREE AGES OF DISABILITY

In attempting a study of the social responses which have been made to handicap, one is faced at the outset with the problem of deciding who is to be regarded as handicapped. Unless we can be clear who we include in the term 'handicapped people' we cannot distinguish those policies which are orientated towards their needs from social policies with a different focus. Yet there are a number of factors which may handicap individuals in some or all aspects of life, such as a prison record, a poor education, a timid disposition, poverty, a large family, being a member of a minority group, or disablement.

Any person experiencing exceptional difficulty in coping with life, due to any one or a combination of factors such as those above, may be said to be handicapped, and social policies to mitigate poverty, rehabilitate ex-offenders, improve housing, expand educational facilities or promote racial and religious tolerance, may then all be seen as part of the social response to handicap.

The focus of this book, however, is much narrower than this. It concentrates on handicap which is the result of disabling disease, recognized functional disorder, injury or congenital defect, and on the social policies designed to affect the lives of people thus disabled.

Although, by taking this focus, we limit the field of concern, definitional problems still remain because there is no clear dividing line between those conditions of body or mind which constitute a handicap and those which do not. After all, a number of people have bodily defects, such as short sight, misshapen feet or missing teeth, but by no means all defects are regarded as handicapping. Similarly we have people ranged across very wide spectrums of intellectual ability and emotional stability. Relatively few are regarded as beyond the limits of what can be accepted as normal. There is no clear, objective and unambiguous distinction between the point where normality ends and disability begins. This is true in respect of physical function, and doubly true with regard to mental or emotional conditions.

The lack of agreement over what constitutes a handicapping disability profoundly affects the confidence with which any estimates of the numbers of handicapped people can be accepted. The best known estimate for Britain is that made by the Office of Population Censuses and Surveys in 1971.[1] The figures produced by that study were the result of scrupulously careful research, and a clear statement of what, for the purposes of that work, was to be regarded as a handicapping condition.

A distinction was drawn between impairment, which was defined as the loss of part or all of a limb, or any defect of organ or mechanism of the body; disability, which was the lack of function which resulted directly from the impairment; and handicap, which was the limitation on normal activities of self-care and mobility consequent upon the loss of function caused by impairment. Thus the survey was able to estimate that there were some three million impaired adults living in private households in Great Britain, but in the case of two-thirds of these individuals their impairment was deemed to be no handicap in the spheres of self-care and getting about. Just over a million of all the impaired people identified were found to be handicapped, according to the definition of the term used by the Office of Population Censuses and Surveys.

To take incompetence in matters of self-care as the defining characteristic of physical or mental handicap offers a workable, if narrow, boundary within which to identify the disabled population. Using this definition, however, we could not identify all the children with mental or physical defects whose childhood activities were restricted, nor all the adults with impairments who were experiencing difficulties in their lives as a result. A different definition of handicap is needed to identify the much larger numbers of disabled people who, while capable of self-care and getting about, are handicapped in other areas of life, but it is practically impossible to agree on what is to be regarded as normal functional ability in spheres other than self-care, departure from which constitutes disability.

For example, running might be a normal activity among twelve-year-old children, so that one of them unable to run would be handicapped, but it is not a normal activity for ninety-year-olds. Is it, to take further the example of running, a normal activity for men and women of, say, forty, such that inability to run because of shortness of breath, or a touch of rheumatism, or a damaged knee cartilage, can be regarded as a handicap? Or do we decide that, at the age of forty, most adults have given up energetic sports or running around from sheer exuberance of energy, so that someone who cannot run is really at no disadvantage – is not, therefore, handicapped although he may have an impairment? We may want to argue the point, and say that while most women of forty are unlikely to be doing much running, a number of men of that age still want to play cricket or be otherwise very active, so that inability to run in a man of forty could be regarded as a handicap, when the same lack of capacity in a woman of that age would not.

No doubt this hypothetical argument could be continued still further, pointing out that nowadays women may be as concerned as their menfolk about remaining highly active – at least in western civilization – but probably enough has been said to demonstrate the fact that normality, and what constitutes a handicap by contrast, varies with age, sex and cultural expectations. It is extremely difficult to identify activities common to mankind, irrespective of individual circumstances, place in the life cycle and social traditions, other than the basic and essential daily living activities, such as eating, excreting, getting into and out of bed, and attending to one's toilet.

In the absence of such agreement, the development of social policy for handicapped people has been based on the most common, most evident and most objectively measured activity undertaken by a group, which is education among children and, among adults; employment, at least for those of working age. Among the elderly population, social policies in general recognize as disabled only those whose physical or mental defects render them incapable of basic self-care.

THE PLAN OF THE BOOK

It is for this reason that it makes sense to examine measures to help handicapped people in the context of a tripartite division between children, adults of working age, and the elderly. Many of the social policies which are discussed in this book are framed with these age groups of the disabled population in mind, and the organization of the book follows the same pattern. We also follow the practice of much of the legislation in this field and for the most part use the terms 'disability' and 'handicap' (and their derivatives) interchangeably.

The next two chapters deal with social policies in respect of disabled children. These are succeeded by an examination of measures to help handicapped adults of working age, followed by a review of the position concerning elderly disabled people. Sometimes, as will be seen particularly in the discussion of services for elderly disabled people, this categorization into broad age-groups of disability leads to anomalies and inappropriate provision. In making use of the three administrative categories of disablement, therefore, we do not overlook the fact that for the individuals concerned the meaning of disability rarely fits in to these neat divisions. We recognize that the way an individual experiences his disability is very much affected by the attitudes of others towards him. It has been cogently argued that anyone with a mental or physical disability is stigmatized by society, which sees his functional impairments as a badge of general imperfection and inadequacy.[2] Indeed, it is sometimes claimed that stigma is, for many disabled people, the major component of their difficulties, frustrations and despair.

Chapter 9 therefore discusses reasons for the failure of social policy to effect, or even really to attempt, a change in public attitudes in the direction of attaching more value to what a disabled person can do than to what he is unable to do. The chapter identifies an overall emphasis on, firstly, helping disabled people to minimize their functional incapacities and be independent or, failing this, secondly to provide fairly minimal succour, and these priorities are then related to the way in which social policy has developed as a concomitant of industrial growth rather than as a challenge to the primacy of rational economic development. The concept of economic rationality in relation to social policy is more fully developed and examined in the last chapter of the book.

Extracts from important and relevant documents to which reference is made in the text are given at the end of the book, followed by chronological lists of enactments, Royal Commissions and enquiry reports. Finally a select bibliography listing a number of the main publications on the topic of social policies for handicapped people appears on pages 184–188.

NOTES AND REFERENCES

1. A. I. HARRIS, *Handicapped and Impaired in Great Britain*, HMSO, London (1971).
2. E. GOFFMAN, *Stigma*, Prentice Hall, New York (1963).

Chapter two

HANDICAPPED SCHOOLCHILDREN

ESTIMATING THE NUMBERS OF HANDICAPPED CHILDREN

Handicapped children form a small proportion of the total number of handicapped people in our society. Physical handicap and psychiatric handicap (as distinct from mental subnormality) are both associated with advancing age, and our disabled population is heavily concentrated among the middle-aged and elderly groups.

None the less there are significant numbers, not very accurately known, of handicapped children. Some are disabled by disease or accident during childhood, and some are born with a physical or mental defect – the congenitally disabled. Some birth defects are so gross as to be immediately visible, as, for example, cases of spina bifida, severe cerebral palsy and Down's syndrome, but there are less obvious but still disabling birth defects which often go undetected for many months, even years.[1] It is therefore impossible to give any precise figure of the numbers of handicapped infants, but the figures for handicapped schoolchildren are more reliable. Even here, however, there is uncertainty, since a special screening in one educational area revealed a number of hitherto undetected disabilities in the children examined, some of which had quite seriously handicapping effects.[2]

Children were not included in the survey of handicapped and impaired people conducted by the Office of Population Censuses and Surveys referred to in Chapter 1,[3] as it was apparently assumed that education statistics were already collected which would suffice to assess numbers of handicapped schoolchildren. The definitions of handicap which have been used in compiling education statistics have not been clearly articulated in official publications[4] and uncertainty about the way in which handicap has been defined only emphasizes the caution which must be employed in any consideration involving the numbers of handicapped children in Britain.

With this caution in mind, the numbers of handicapped schoolchildren have been estimated to be in the region of 180,000, half of them mentally handicapped.[5] In addition there is an unknown number of handicapped infants below school age. A very rough estimate of the number of these may be arrived at by assuming that there is no marked variation in the numbers of handicapped children from year to year, in which case the 180,000 handicapped children spread over the eleven years of school life from 5 to 16 represent approximately 16,000 in each year. If this is projected backwards from the age of 5 to birth, one arrives at an estimate of about 80,000 handicapped under five years old. This is a very crude estimate indeed, but may serve as a rough indication of the numbers involved.

THE ORIGINS OF COLLECTIVE PROVISION FOR HANDICAPPED CHILDREN

The fact that handicapped youngsters have special needs has long been recognized. Most early provision to meet these needs was by religious or charitable bodies but, as early as 1601, Queen Elizabeth I passed a Poor Law which encouraged parish officials to give some training for employment to blind or crippled children. Similar encouragement to Parish Guardians to help handicapped young people to obtain education and training for work was contained, two hundred years later, in the Poor Law Reform Act 1834. Neither statute had much success in ensuring that special care was taken to meet the educational and training needs of handicapped children.

The first really effective step in this direction came when a Royal Commission, appointed to enquire into the condition of the blind, the deaf and dumb, and the mentally handicapped, reported in 1889 strongly urging the necessity to improve educational provision for handicapped children.[6] The Commission noted that, apart from some charitable institutions and schools, very little was being done for handicapped children, and in its report it recommended that the state should accept responsibility for the education of blind, deaf and dumb, and 'feeble-minded' or retarded children. The report observed: 'It is better for the local authority or the State to expend its funds on the elementary and technical education of the blind and the deaf, etc. for a few years rather than have to support them through life in idleness.'[7] This clear statement of the economic rationality of making special provision for handicapped children brought swift results. In 1893 the Elementary Education (Blind and Deaf Children) Act reached the statute-book, followed in 1899, after further investigation regarding mentally handicapped children,[8] by the Elementary Education (Defective and Epileptic Children) Act.

EDUCATION FOR HANDICAPPED CHILDREN

The above two Acts represented the first effective involvement by the state in the problems of handicapped children. The Act concerning blind and deaf children imposed firm obligations on local education authorities to make special provision for these groups of handicapped children. With regard to defective and severely epileptic children, local education authorities were empowered to make special provision if they considered it necessary or desirable.

The type of special provision to be offered was not specified in any detail. There were several special schools for blind children already in existence, and a few for deaf children, run by voluntary charitable organizations. It was apparently anticipated that the education authorities would utilize these facilities in the discharge of their obligations under the Elementary Education (Blind and Deaf Children) Act. Where such facilities did not exist or were inadequate, the Report of the Royal Commission was not at all insistent on education authorities establishing special schools or even special classes exclusively for blind children, providing that some teaching to use braille was available to the blind pupils. It was assumed, however, that deaf children could not benefit from being incorporated in ordinary schools.

It is interesting to see here the early emergence of an issue which is still debated, as to whether or not the special educational needs of handicapped children can best be met in ordinary schools with the mainstream of children, or in specially equipped and staffed segregated schools.

The Elementary Education (Defective and Epileptic Children) Act conferred on local education authorities the power to do what the biggest and best (London) had already begun to do – provide special schools or classes for mentally subnormal children. Moberley, the Chairman of the London School Board, had argued since 1880 that if mentally retarded children were to reach their full potential, they needed to be taught at a slower pace and in smaller classes than would be possible by merely absorbing them in ordinary schools. In his view, it was short-sighted economy which encouraged most School Boards to admit retarded children to ordinary schools rather than set up special schools to cater for their special needs.

Moberley's argument contrasts with the popular modern view, where admission of handicapped children to ordinary schools is hailed as progress rather than parsimony, and the whole concept of special provision is under attack as isolationist and unsympathetic. This campaign, it is true, focuses mainly on the desirability of admitting physically handicapped children to ordinary schools, and there has so far been less agitation to reduce or eliminate special provision for mentally handicapped schoolchildren.

In fact, neither of the first two Acts referred to above paid much attention to children with physical handicaps other than sensory or severe epilepsy. The view was expressed at the time that physical defect alone did not justify admission of a child to a special class or school. It is possible that, in the 1890s, children with severe physical defects seldom survived long enough to require schooling, or perhaps it was merely assumed that any physically disabled child who could not cope in the ordinary school environment was most certainly unemployable whether educated or not, so that special school provision would be a waste of money.

Despite the fact that most physically handicapped children were officially expected to sink or swim in the ordinary school system without any special help, several local education authorities began to make use of their permissive powers under the Act of 1899 and established special schools for physically defective children who could not be accommodated in the ordinary Board School environment. In addition, some charitable organizations established a few schools to take severely physically handicapped children who could not cope in the ordinary schools. We shall never know how many disabled children benefited from the opportunities thus created, nor how many others were denied schooling because of lack of special school places. Undoubtedly there were some handicapped children who never managed to obtain any form of schooling; probably there were many.

Within a few years it was recognized that special educational provision for mentally and physically handicapped children could not be left as a matter of choice for local education authorities under legislation which was merely permissive. The war of 1914–18 delayed the introduction of social legislation, but the Education

Act passed in 1918 took a further step in providing educational opportunities for disabled children. The Act made mandatory the provision of special educational facilities which local authorities had merely been permitted to provide under the Act of 1899, and extended the requirement to include physically handicapped children.

This was a comprehensive measure and encouraged the expansion of facilities for handicapped children. It set the broad policy lines which Education Acts in the next fifty years were to follow, although the detail with which categories of handicap were specified varied from five groups in the early part of the period to eleven groups in the Education Act 1944, subsequently reduced to ten categories. Throughout this time, however, the needs of one group of children continued to be ignored – those of the severely mentally subnormal.

BRINGING SEVERELY MENTALLY HANDICAPPED CHILDREN INTO THE EDUCATIONAL SYSTEM

The Elementary Education (Defective and Epileptic Children) Act 1899 had drawn a distinction between mentally defective children who were, and those who were not, capable of benefiting from education. The distinction was imprecise and practice did nothing to clarify the issue. With the introduction of intelligence testing an arbitrary decision was made as to the score which would distinguish the subnormal but educable child from the severely subnormal and so-called ineducable child. Even this questionable criterion was not applied impartially, as parental pressure and the doctor's subjective impressions of the child and his family were allowed to enter into the decision as to whether or not a particular child was ineducable.[9] The Education (Handicapped Children) Act 1970 finally abandoned the practice of certifying some children as ineducable, and charged local education authorities with the responsibility for the education of *all* handicapped children.

Ending the system of certifying as ineducable those children of severely subnormal intelligence removed one cause of considerable distress to the parents of such children. For years, any parents aware of the significance of the label had used every ounce of influence and persuasion at their command to avoid having their handicapped child written off as ineducable and fit only for special day-centre attendance or custodial care in one of the large mental institutions. A key person in the battles waged over the future of the child was the doctor, who thus found himself with the conflicting responsibilities of supporting and assisting the parents in the management and fullest possible development of their seriously handicapped child, and acting as the judge who condemned the child as unsuitable for education in school. The inclination of most doctors was to certify as few children as possible as ineducable, with the result that special school places for educationally retarded children were heavily over-subscribed, while some National Health Service training sections, intended for the ineducable children who were not admitted to the educational system, were under-utilized.

The Act of 1970 therefore had two aims – ending a questionable practice of distinction between educable and ineducable children which had caused distress to parents and professionals alike and was not in the interests of the children concerned; and making more flexible and rational use of the educational and training facilities available for the mentally subnormal child. Some 30,000 children who had been the responsibility of the health authorities came into the educational system after the Act. The transfer of responsibility did not necessarily mean any transfer of physical location for these children, who mostly continued to attend the same day centre or unit in the hospital complex as before the Act. None the less, the acceptance of responsibility by the education service marked recognition of the fact that the best, if not the only, treatment for mental handicap was education in its broadest sense.

A mentally handicapped child not only has a lower ceiling of potential development (though this has in very many cases been kept lower than it need be due to lack of stimulation and opportunity) but he also learns more slowly and has less capacity for learning incidentally in play, by observation, or from experience. It follows, therefore, that the more seriously mentally handicapped a child is, the greater is his need for education to maximize his competence. This conclusion, reached by growing numbers of those concerned with mentally handicapped children, underlies the change of responsibility for severely subnormal children from the National Health Service to the educational services effected by the Education (Handicapped Children) Act 1970.

The provisions of this Act only became operative in 1971, shortly before Britain was affected by increasing and severe economic problems, reflected in restrictions and later reductions in public spending. It is difficult, therefore, to estimate the extent to

which the transfer of responsibility for mentally handicapped children has improved their educational opportunities, nor is there much factual material available on which to base such an assessment. Peter Mittler, Director of the Hester Adrian Research Centre for the study of the development of mentally handicapped children, writing in 1978, thought there had been considerable progress since 1971.[10] He based his judgement on the facts that:
(i) fewer mentally handicapped children were without a school place of any kind (although there were still some in this unhappy situation);
(ii) the percentage of teachers of severely subnormal children possessing appropriate qualifications had increased from one-third to 80 per cent; and
(iii) economic stringency had affected special education less than it had other spheres of the educational services, showing the importance which education authorities attached to improving educational provision for children of severely subnormal intelligence.

TEACHERS OF HANDICAPPED CHILDREN

As teaching is regarded as a professional skill for which an intensive training over several years is required, then it might be supposed that to teach children who had special needs or special learning difficulties would demand an even higher level of training. The actual status of teachers in special units, however, does not support this supposition.

Teachers of blind children and of deaf children were required under Regulation 15 (2) of the Handicapped Pupils and Special Schools Regulations 1959 to have special qualifications in addition to an ordinary teacher's certificate. Teachers of other groups of handicapped children are expected to hold a teacher's certificate, and to have had some experience of teaching normal children, but are not required to have any special training to equip them to deal with the learning needs of their handicapped pupils.

Among teachers in ordinary schools, an increasing proportion in recent years have held degrees as well as the teacher's certificate, but the proportion of teachers in special schools with this higher level of qualifications is much smaller than among teachers in ordinary schools. This suggests that teaching in special schools does not attract the most academically able teachers, indicating that teaching handicapped children is not widely recognized as demanding special attributes and given an accordingly high status and prestige. An enquiry among student teachers in 1972 confirmed that few of them were willing to teach handicapped children[11] and another study found that practising teachers accorded little prestige to those employed in special schools.[12]

Some of the explanation for this lack of prestige attaching to the teaching of handicapped children may arise from the fact that teaching is often regarded primarily as a matter of equipping pupils to pass academic examinations at the highest possible level. This is a very narrow view, and one that has been criticized in the context of ordinary schooling for the way it favours the intellectually able few and denigrates the majority of children who are, by definition, of only average ability. Yet it is a function of education likely to be emphasized in the future now that each school is required to provide information on its examination achievements. The importance attached to examination success has particularly unfortunate consequences for mentally handicapped children, and even for children of normal intellectual capacity whose physical defects interrupt or impede learning, as it accentuates the reluctance of the most able and ambitious teachers to enter the special education field, with its poor examination prospects. This further depresses the opportunities in special schools of those children who could aspire to academic qualifications.

The severely mentally handicapped child, as has been seen, was for a long time excluded altogether from the educational system on the grounds that he could not benefit from education in the narrow sense of being taught academic skills. When the regulations had been framed in 1959 concerning the qualifications required of staff in special schools, the severely subnormal children were still outside the educational system, and there was no requirement for staff in National Health Service junior training units to have any qualifications at all for the supremely difficult and demanding job of teaching very severely, often multiply handicapped children, many of whom are unable to use or understand language. Yet research has shown that there are ways of stimulating even the most profoundly handicapped, thus actively fostering their development.[13] The skills to do this need to be learned, but there were few opportunities until the 1960s for staff involved with severely subnormal children to obtain any training at all for their important work. The National Association of Mental Health, a voluntary body, was first in the field and established some two-year training courses for teachers of the mentally handicapped. In

1964 the Ministry of Health (to become part of the Department of Health and Social Security in 1966) formed the Training Council for Teachers of the Mentally Handicapped, which encouraged the development in colleges of the two-year specialized training course. The work of this Council in promoting the training of teachers ended after the Education Act 1970 whereby the education of mentally handicapped children was made the responsibility of education authorities, and therefore the training of teachers for them became the responsibility of the Department of Education and Science.

The proportion of teachers of mentally handicapped children holding a basic qualification increased rapidly during the late 1960s and the 1970s. Few, however, held an ordinary teacher's certificate as well as a specialist qualification for teaching handicapped children. There are a few colleges of education where teachers in training for the teacher's certificate can take a specialist option in the teaching of handicapped children, but these courses have been criticized for failing to give sufficient weight to the specialist training. A report of a Committee of Inquiry into the education of handicapped children, published in 1978, expressed reservations about the adequacy of the existing facilities for training teachers of the mentally handicapped,[14] and clearly much remains to be done to equip an adequate number of teachers with sufficient skills to make education, in its widest sense, fully available to severely mentally handicapped children, as was envisaged in the Education Act 1970.

THE CONTROVERSY OVER SPECIAL SCHOOLS FOR HANDICAPPED PUPILS

This issue has already been touched upon as it arose in connection with the earliest state measures to promote educational opportunities for handicapped children. The matter was not debated in the 1890s in terms of integration and segregation, as it tends to be today, but more in terms of whether expenditure on special educational facilities for certain groups of handicapped children was either necessary or likely to be useful in equipping them for employment.

The first groups of handicapped children to be seen as warranting special educational provision were the blind and the deaf and dumb, followed by the educationally subnormal and those with epilepsy. In 1918 other groups of handicapped children were specified as needing special educational consideration and provision, and the process was finally completed in 1970 when severely mentally subnormal children became a group for which the education authorities had a statutory responsibility to provide schooling.

Even before the final group was included in 1970, pressure was growing to reduce, or end, special school provision for handicapped children and instead to design and organize the ordinary school environment in such a way as to make it capable of including practically all handicapped children. The Acts which had encouraged the provision of special educational facilities had always allowed for the fact that as many handicapped children as could manage in ordinary schools would be admitted to them, leaving only those who would otherwisc not be able to receive an education to be accommodated in special schools or special classes.

It was possible, however, that the existence of special facilities encouraged school authorities to draw narrower limits of the variation in intellectual and physical competence which was acceptable in an ordinary school, secure in the knowledge that there were special schools for any child rejected as outside these limits. Many children who could have managed perfectly well in an ordinary school, although handicapped, may thus have been denied the opportunity to do so and forced instead to attend a special school with all the disadvantages of being isolated from the generality of their peers.

Certainly some children have attended special schools who could have coped with an ordinary school environment[15] and it is possible that this happened more frequently in the period before public and parental pressure against the use of special schools became vocal. It must also be said, however, that some handicapped children may now be attending ordinary school when their development might be better promoted in an environment which offered special facilities.[16]

Concern over the best way to meet the special educational needs of handicapped children led to a Committee of Inquiry being established in 1974 under the chairmanship of Mrs Mary Warnock, Fellow of Lady Margaret Hall, Oxford. This Committee took four years to complete its work, and before its report appeared in 1978[17] the government took action and passed the Education Act 1976. Section 10 of this Act required education authorities to accommodate handicapped children in ordinary schools except in cases where it would be quite impracticable, would involve unreasonable expense, or would be clearly against the best interests of the child concerned [doc 1]. Section 10, therefore, made admission to an ordinary school the appropriate course for every handicapped child unless there were very strong reasons against doing so. This part of the Education Act 1976, however, was not to come into effect until a date determined by the Secretary of State for Education, and in the event it never was implemented, as the Conservative government which took office in 1979 rejected the intention of section 10 and introduced its own proposals for meeting special educational needs [doc 2].[18]

The Warnock Committee of Inquiry had taken account of section 10 and treated it as a *fait accompli* which pre-empted any further debate on the advantages or disadvantages of admitting disabled children to ordinary schools. Consequently the Committee concentrated instead on the practical measures which could be taken to ensure that the special educational needs of handicapped children would be met, whether in ordinary or special schools.

A major point made by the Warnock Report was that disability constituted only one cause of special educational need. There were other causes, such as frequent moves of school, emotional disturbance, unfamiliarity with the English language, or adverse home conditions. The Committee estimated that as many as one in five of all children experienced some learning difficulty from one cause or another, and suggested that there was no good reason to separate out for special treatment only those whose difficulties were caused by mental or physical handicap. What was needed, the Warnock Report declared, was a system for assessing, and then trying to meet, the special needs of any schoolchild observed to have some learning difficulty, from whatever cause.

Some system of assessment had, of course, been implied by section 10 of the Education Act 1976, as there needed to be some way of deciding when it would be impracticable, unreasonably expensive, or against the child's best interests, to admit any particular handicapped child to an ordinary school. This would require a careful assessment of the child's needs and capabilities in order to determine the type of special help, if any, he would need, and whether this could reasonably be made available at the ordinary neighbourhood school. The Warnock proposals for greater co-ordination of the professionals involved in assessing and assisting handicapped children were intended as practical suggestions for the effective implementation of section 10.

Response to the Warnock Report was generally favourable, but a general election intervened and it was not until 1980 that the new government produced its proposals for implementing the recommendations of the Report [doc 2]. These included the announcement that section 10 of the 1976 Act would not be implemented. Instead, local education authorities were to be asked to make provision for all pupils with special educational needs. It was accepted that most children thus identified as having special needs would be in ordinary schools and would continue to receive their education in the ordinary school system. A small minority, expected to correspond roughly to the total of those children who had previously been identified as disabled in the ten separate categories of handicap, were to have a legal status, involving being 'recorded' by the local educational authority as having special educational needs. The decision whether or not to record a child was to be taken formally by the local authority on the basis of professional assessment of the child and having regard to the views of the child's parents, who had the right of appeal against the local authority's decision.

A 'recorded' child would be educated in an ordinary school provided the facilities were adequate, that such a placement would be compatible with the efficient education of other children and with the use of public resources, and had regard to the wishes of the parents. Parents could appeal to the Secretary of State if they did not like the school chosen for their child by the local educational authority, but would have to show that a placement in the school of their choice would meet the three criteria of adequate facilities, moderate commitment of resources, and compatibility with the efficient education of the other children in the school. In other words, although parents of 'recorded' children were to be given the same right to express preferences as was conferred on the parents of non-'recorded' children in the Education Act 1980, their choice would only be met under certain specific conditions which had more to do with efficient economy than with the desires and interests of the handicapped child and his parents. This is an important rider, since, from the views expressed by associations representing parents of handicapped children and by handicapped persons themselves, it is clear that parents of disabled children overwhelmingly prefer them to attend ordinary schools. This reflects the parents' conviction that special schools as presently constituted do not usually offer handicapped children better opportunities than are available to them in ordinary schools, despite the difficulties and disadvantages often entailed.

The government, therefore, acknowledged the fact, emphasized in the Warnock Report, that special educational needs exist in many more children than the relatively small number who have a mental or physical handicap. Beyond charging local authorities to have regard to these needs, however, the government offered no additional resources and proposed to do virtually nothing in respect of the majority of children identified as having special educational needs. Physically and mentally handicapped children continued to be given a separate emphasis and legal recognition, but such children were in future to be identified on one comprehensive record, rather than in ten separate categories according to type of disablement. Any benefits of this change are likely to be in the sphere of administrative efficiency and economy rather than in improvements in the educational opportunities of disabled schoolchildren.

INTEGRATION AND EDUCATION

The government's interpretation of the recommendations of the Warnock Report, and the rejection of section 10 of the Education Act 1976, suggests that children identified as having special educational needs due to physical or mental handicap will continue to have much the same chance as before – no less and no more – of being educated in ordinary schools. Even before the government's intentions were made clear in 1980, doubts had grown about the official will to implement section 10. A major factor determining whether or not it is practicable for a physically disabled child to attend an ordinary school is the design of the buildings. At the time of passing the 1976 Act the then government gave an undertaking, in response to pressure in the House of Lords from Baroness d'Arcy de Knayth, herself disabled, to amend the Standard for School Premises Regulations 1972 and the Further Education Regulations 1975 in order to ensure that school buildings would be made accessible to the handicapped. This was not done, and when in 1980 Baroness d'Arcy de Knayth questioned the delay she was told by a spokesman for the Conservative government which had been returned in 1979 that, for technical reasons, the regulations could not be amended in the way earlier envisaged.[19]

Much of the opposition to special schools for handicapped children centres on the argument that a handicapped child in a special school is segregated from his peers, while that same child in an ordinary school would be integrated into the local child community. A growing number of people, including many parents of disabled children, have pressed for 'integration in education' by which they mean the inclusion of handicapped children in the ordinary school system. There were also, of course, those who warned that too simplistic a view was being taken of what constituted integration. Peter Mittler, with years of research experience into the best ways of promoting the development of handicapped children, declares:

> ... the assumption is made that special schools 'segregate' and normal schools 'integrate'. But the issues are far more complex than this. Not only is there a whole range of provision from extreme segregation to total integration, but a school which may at first sight appear to fall at one extreme or the other in terms of its 'label', may, in fact be operating very differently in real terms. For example, a class of handicapped children attached to an infant school may in practice never work or play with normal children and lead a segregated existence in all but name; similarly even when a special school is on the same campus as a normal school, there need not necessarily be any contact between staff or children. A residential school in a remote rural area may become fully part of the community, and its pupils accepted as local children. A handicapped child may even be in an ordinary classroom every day but may be isolated socially and educationally from other children and from the activities of the class. ... Merely placing handicapped children in a normal school does not guarantee that any social or educational integration will take place.[20]

To put a child who has special needs in a school environment which is geared to meet only the ordinary needs of children is to put the handicapped child at a disadvantage. If the special needs created by his handicap are slight, or are not such as to affect many of the normal school activities engaged in by his classmates, then there is every reason to include him in an ordinary school, where he may compensate for less than average performance in one area by a better than average performance in another. His handicap will remain, and may continue to affect his relationship with his non-handicapped school fellows to some extent, but there will be a range of activities where his performance is at least as good as theirs, and where he displays no special difficulties or needs. If there are sufficient of these successful areas to ensure that most of the time, in most ways, his performance is average, he will probably be socially and educationally integrated into the ordinary school community. For such a child it may be agreed that it would be a disservice to place him in any special school or class, however good.

On the other hand, a child whose handicap presents difficulties for him in a number of school activities such as play, listening, reciting, manual dexterity, writing, memorizing, sport and so on, is going to be unable to compete on equal terms in most if not all areas of performance. His special needs are likely to be so apparent that, even if special efforts are made to meet them, he remains isolated on the fringe of the ordinary school group. He is, moreover, condemned to a continuous and almost total sense of failure because of his inability to keep up with the other children in most of the significant spheres of school activity. In these circumstances there can be little if any integration of the child into the ordinary life of the school, let alone into the hobbies or play of the children out of school, and he may well be happier and more confident of his abilities and worth in a good special school or class environment.

This seems so obvious that one must ask why so many parents of even severely disabled children will, if given the opportunity, choose to expose their handicapped youngsters to the stresses and disappointments of coping with an ordinary school, apparently in the name of such a dubious form of integration. One clearly cannot dismiss all such parents as misguided. A more likely explanation is that special schools are seen by many parents of handicapped children not as enhancing a child's educational development but as retarding it even more than is likely in an ordinary school despite the difficulties. Consequently education in an ordinary school is seen as offering the best chance at present available for the child to reach his maximum potential – and the greater his educational development, the better chance he will have of a measure of integration into society as an adult.

No doubt some special schools are excellent, but in general the lack of prestige attaching to special school teaching in the eyes of most teachers is matched by the lack of esteem in which such schools are held by the public, and particularly by those whose children encounter them. Neither teachers nor public will be persuaded to a different view unless the allocation of resources to special education is sufficiently high to make it special in the sense of being specially advantageous, rather than simply segregated from the ordinary school system. Expenditure on education services generally, however, tends to be geared to the projected needs of the labour market – if the demand for technologists is rising, for example, then resources will be concentrated on developing scientific education rather than the classics or the arts.

This, of course, is understandable, since no country could afford to devote the very considerable amounts spent on education if the result was to equip the children with skills which were inappropriate to the jobs which needed to be filled in order to keep the society viable. On the other hand, it has meant in the past, and will doubtless mean in the future, that educational services for those not likely to participate in the labour force have a low priority. This applies to special education for severely handicapped children. In present circumstances, parents are making a realistic appraisal of the balance of educational advantages when they exert all the influence they possess to get their handicapped children into ordinary schools if at all possible.

It is not realistic, however, to expect that sufficient resources will be forthcoming to pay for alterations, additional equipment or special assistance in order to modify significantly the ordinary school environment so as to facilitate the admission of severely disabled children. To do this would be more expensive than effecting quite considerable improvements in special schools – and even these are only to be expected when resources are plentiful for education services generally and the special schools come in for their share. In the economic gloom of the 1980s there is not likely to be a significant increase in resources for educational services generally, nor can one look for any redistribution of resources within the educational sphere from the high spending sectors into the special education services.

NOTES AND REFERENCES

1. M. RUTTER, J. TIZZARD AND K. WHITMORE (eds). *Education, Health and Behaviour*, Longman, London (1970).
2. *Ibid*.
3. A. I. HARRIS, *Handicapped and Impaired in Great Britain*, Office of Population Censuses and Surveys, HMSO, London (1971).
4. Education statistics are published annually in the series *Statistics of Education*, HMSO, London.
5. E. TOPLISS, *Provision for the Disabled* (2nd edn), Basil Blackwell & Martin Robertson, Oxford (1979), p. 30. Peter Mittler, *People not Patients*, Methuen, London (1978) suggests on p. 79 that there are 90,000 mentally handicapped schoolchildren.
6. *Report of the Royal Commission on the Blind, the Deaf and Dumb, etc. of the United Kingdom, 1889*, C 5781, Vol. xix.

7. *Ibid.*
8. *Report of the Departmental Committee on Defective and Epileptic Children 1898*, C 8746, Vol. xxvi.
9. Z.A. STEIN AND M.W. SUSSER, 'Families of dull children', *Journal of Mental Science*, **106**, 1296–319.
10. P. MITTLER, *op. cit.*
11. M. J. TOBIN, 'Attitudes of non-specialist teachers towards visually handicapped pupils', *Teacher of the Blind*, **60**, 60–4.
12. D. SHARPLES AND D. J. THOMAS, 'The perceived prestige of normal and special education teachers', *Exceptional Children*, **35**, 473–9.
13. M. STEVENS, *The Educational and Social Needs of Children with Severe Handicap*, (2nd edn) Edward Arnold, London (1976).
14. *Special Educational Needs, Report of the Committee of Inquiry into the Education of Handicapped Children and Young People*, Cmnd 7212. HMSO, London (1978). (Chairman: Mrs Mary Warnock.)
15. E. M. ANDERSON, *The Disabled Schoolchild*, Methuen, London (1973).
16. *Ibid.* See also *The Health of the School Child 1969–1970, Report of the Chief Medical Officer of the Department of Education and Science*, HMSO, London (1972). Publication of these reports has ceased, and the data for 1969–70 are the most recent available in this form.
17. *Special Educational Needs, op. cit.*
18. *Special Needs in Education*, Cmnd 7996, HMSO, London (1980).
19. *H. L. Deb.* (1980) Vol. 406, cols. 1371–2.
20. P. MITTLER, *op. cit.*, p. 96.

Chapter three

HANDICAPPED AND OUT OF SCHOOL

HANDICAPPED SCHOOL-LEAVERS

Compulsory education for all children, both disabled and able-bodied, finishes at age 16, and after that the majority of children are expected to enter employment. A minority of children go on to higher education (for academic qualifications) or further education (for vocational-type training). The needs of handicapped children get almost no special consideration in after-school arrangements.

However good the school education of a handicapped child and however skilled and dedicated his teachers, the efforts of child, school, teachers and parents are directed towards a near vacuum at the point of leaving school. There is no system by which the potential of each individual handicapped child could be assessed by all those who might be involved in arrangements for his future – head teacher, careers officer, youth employment officer, disablement resettlement officer, social worker, a medical opinion where relevant and, of course, the child himself and his parents.

Social policies to assist the handicapped school-leaver are conspicuous by their absence, although this lack of provision has been noted and criticised in numerous well-informed reports in the past.[1] It was also commented upon in the Warnock Report[2] which made a number of suggestions for improving services for handicapped school-leavers. The government drew these to the attention of local education authorities, while at the same time refusing either to impose a statutory duty to improve provisions, or to make additional resources available to those authorities attempting to comply with the Warnock recommendations. Without a considerable expansion of provision, however, it is likely that future cohorts of handicapped school-leavers will experience the uncertainties and neglect which at present cause so much distress to many disabled youngsters and their families.

Some assessment courses for handicapped school-leavers are organized in a few of the Employment Rehabilitation Centres run by the Manpower Services Commission. These Centres were established by the government with the main function of assisting the employment rehabilitation of the person who had been in employment but had become disabled in adult life due to disease or injury. The Centres are equipped to give advice and practical help to enable a recently disabled adult to adapt to employment conditions again despite diminished capacities. They are not really geared to assessing the potential of a handicapped school-leaver for further education or particular employment avenues, although a few have made special efforts to develop this expertise and can offer assessment courses to selected groups of handicapped school-leavers. Only a minority of disabled youngsters have the opportunity to attend such courses. For the vast majority, school leaving poses a huge question mark of – what next? The answer, too often, is – nothing.

FURTHER AND HIGHER EDUCATIONAL FACILITIES

Physically handicapped school-leavers of normal intelligence might, of course, wish to pursue higher or further educational aims. A number of them manage to do so, but advanced education facilities specially designed or adapted for disabled young people are very sparse, so that most handicapped young people pursuing their education must be able to cope in normal further and higher educational environments. Most of these establishments were never designed to facilitate access by disabled students. Since the Chronically Sick and Disabled Persons Act 1970 [doc 3] educational institutions have been required to have consideration for the needs of disabled people when planning any new building or major adaptations. The Act, however, did not provide for any way of compelling the provision of access facilities if, after consideration, it was decided that to make a building or institution accessible would be too expensive or difficult. The National Bureau for Handicapped Students found that there were still very few handicapped students who managed to gain entry to courses in further and higher educational institutions, and pointed to the lack of facilities which made it impossible for them to cope physically, however able they might be intellectually. More particularly, the Bureau stressed that admissions procedures often had the effect of discriminating, albeit unintentionally, against the applications of handicapped young people.[3]

Further evidence for the fact that it is not intellectual inadequacy or lack of motivation which accounts for the small numbers of physically handicapped students continuing their education in colleges and universities comes from the fact that no less than 1,500 disabled students were following Open University courses in 1980, representing almost 3 per cent of the total Open University enrolment.[4] The Open University courses have the advantage that they can be pursued by the disabled student in the convenience of his own home and, perhaps more importantly, at his own pace. The Open University has also provided a number of special services to facilitate the progress of its disabled students, including making course material available on tapes for blind students, providing for examination answers to be submitted in braille, on tape, or dictated to an amanuensis, and supplying a personal assistant free of charge for disabled students attending the residential Summer School required by many courses.

Few of the traditional centres of further and higher education have made as much effort as the Open University to facilitate study by disabled individuals. Most institutions with residential accommodation for all or part of the student body will give some priority in the allocation of rooms to the needs of any disabled students admitted. A few centres, such as the universities at Birmingham, Brighton and Southampton, have opened specially designed and equipped units to accommodate students too severely handicapped to cope in even the most convenient of ordinary student residences. Apart from the special living accommodation, however, little modification has been made to the campuses generally, including libraries and laboratories, or to teaching and examination arrangements, to assist the disabled students once admitted. This probably explains why the specially designed facilities are under-subscribed while physically handicapped students of high intellectual ability continue to enrol for degree courses with the Open University.

It could be argued that, as long as some opportunities for further study exist for disabled students, it is unnecessary for all institutions of further and higher education to make provision to admit handicapped persons. Quite apart from the limitations on choice of course which such a course of action (or inaction) necessarily imposes on handicapped students, there is also the point that most ordinary students look to their college or university as a place of companionship and recreation, as well as of study. The Open University affords its students only minimal contact with their fellows and with the staff. For the able-bodied student in employment, or with family commitments, who enrols for an Open University course, this may not matter – he has his companionship and recreation available elsewhere. For the disabled student, it represents a narrower form of participation and enjoyment than he could perhaps achieve in a traditional college or university environment.

There are some very severely disabled students whose physical limitations of movement or endurance are so great that even to be in the setting of a college or university would permit them little interaction with fellow students. In these cases the Open University probably offers all that such a heavily handicapped person has the energy, physical capacity and inclination to enjoy. But there are also many other handicapped young people who could enjoy and benefit from pursuing their studies with non-handicapped students if only access to the relevant centres were better and a greater readiness existed to admit disabled students for whom relatively minor modifications in teaching and examination techniques might be necessary.

Arguments for the expansion of higher and further educational opportunities for handicapped students have most often been couched in terms of affording the disabled young person a better quality of life – rather than in terms of preparing them for employment, which may remain unlikely however well educated a seriously handicapped young person becomes. While many people may be prepared to accept the desirability of a handicapped youngster acquiring the highest level of educational achievement of which he is capable, even if only to enable him the better to enjoy his leisure, far fewer will accord this objective priority over other uses of scarce resources in the field of higher education. When competition for resources is acute, as at the present time, funds are likely to be committed to those areas of expenditure where some benefit to society as a whole may be expected to accrue – to measures, for example, which promise to produce more young people better equipped to fill crucial gaps in the labour force, thus improving the nation's economic prospects. The absence of any obvious return to the community to be anticipated by improving higher educational opportunities for handicapped students may explain the tardy expansion of facilities.

FURTHER TRAINING FOR THE MENTALLY HANDICAPPED

For the severely mentally handicapped young person, the usual further and higher educational courses are irrelevant, and yet there is good reason to believe that many of them, too, could benefit considerably from opportunities for further development. The slowness of learning which is the defining characteristic of mental handicap makes prolonged education obviously desirable for young people with this condition. Many of them at present finish schooling simply because they have reached the chronological age of 16, although the average mental age of mentally handicapped school-leavers is between 5 and 6 – the age when schooling begins for the ordinary child! Moreover, many severely subnormal children only begin to make marked development in competence in the final year or two of their school life, reflecting the slowness of their ability to respond to teaching.[5]

Despite the indications that many mentally handicapped children could benefit from continuing education after the age of 16, for most of them at present there is only the prospect of an Adult Training Centre, if a place is available. The emphasis on the development of individual skills and competence in these centres is not great, probably because the staff in them generally hold very low expectations of those attending them. According to some studies, there is a considerable degree of under-estimation of handicapped people in Adult Training Centres, with a corresponding level of under-achievement.[6]

There are still some mentally handicapped school-leavers who cannot even find a place in an Adult Training Centre. These simply leave school at sixteen with no future daily activity plans at all. This is a situation of considerable stress and anxiety for the families concerned, because the whole burden of twenty-four-hour-a-day care and supervision falls on the parents, most usually the mother alone for the major part of the time. The handicapped person often becomes bored and can regress and become disruptive. The mother's routine of previous years, based on her child's regular daily excursions to school, is completely disorganized, and any activity or employment outside the home which she may have had usually ceases, with consequent restriction of her interests and possible financial loss to the family. It is not surprising, therefore, that this is a period of crisis for many families which leads in a number of cases to demands that the handicapped member be admitted to institutional care.

Once again, the absence of any comprehensive assessment of the potential and needs of the handicapped school-leaver is seen to create a situation where the individual and his family feel isolated with their problem. It must be admitted, however, that while good assessment procedures might reassure handicapped individuals and their families that others were concerned, in order to be really constructive a range of opportunities must exist to permit a choice of outcome for the handicapped school-leaver. At present, although there have been some hopeful local initiatives, such as organizing enclaves of sheltered work in open employment for handicapped people, there is depressingly little variety of activity open to the mentally handicapped school-leaver.

INTO EMPLOYMENT

The majority of severely mentally handicapped schoolchildren at present go on to Adult Training Centres. Some of the less severely handicapped enter sheltered employment, and an infinitesimal number find jobs on the open market, although, with better training and improved assessment and placing procedures, more could do useful work.

Employment prospects for physically disabled youngsters are better, although most of those with any appreciable degree of handicap experience great difficulty in finding employment in the open market. This is despite the Disabled Persons (Employment) Act 1944 which imposed on all employers of twenty or more workers the obligation to recruit up to 3 per cent of their labour force from disabled people on the employment register [doc 4]. This quota system is not routinely observed, and job opportunities for those with more than a mild handicap are not good; they become even worse at times of high unemployment among able-bodied workers.

Sheltered workshops, as well as accommodating some of the less profoundly mentally handicapped young people, also offer employment to some physically handicapped school-leavers, but the range of work tasks in these workshops is very limited and not intellectually demanding or satisfying. The workshops operate under the aegis of the employment services and are intended to cover their costs. To this end, only those capable of at least one-third the output of an able-bodied worker can expect to be employed. This rules out the most heavily disabled people whose incapacities make this level of output unattainable.

For a severely physically handicapped youngster, the end of schooldays can mean the beginning of virtual imprisonment in his own home, with companionship, stimulation and occupation limited to what the family members can provide. As in the case of those mentally handicapped school-leavers unable to secure a place in an Adult Training Centre, the complete dependence on the resources of the family often provokes considerable tension and distress and can precipitate institutional admission.

In a period of high unemployment, such as at the beginning of the 1980s, when agencies of the Manpower Services Commission are very concerned about the poor job prospects of able-bodied school-leavers, there are few resources left over to devote to improving the opportunities of the difficult-to-place handicapped young person. The outlook is bleak for the employment of appreciably disabled young people, and the cuts in education and social services budgets make the provision of alternative educational and recreational opportunities most unlikely.

LEAVING HOME

Most disabled children live with their families. Even among the special school population, the numbers attending as day pupils far outweigh those in boarding schools – and in a number of these latter, pupils board only during the week, returning home for weekends and holidays. To this extent, the lives of handicapped children are little different from those of other children. Only a tiny minority of very severely, usually multiply, handicapped children grow up in an institutional setting. For handicapped children, as for other children, family life is generally accepted as natural and desirable wherever possible. There is, however, a very different attitude towards leaving home at the end of childhood according to whether the young person is disabled or not.

Increasing numbers of young adults today want and expect to leave the parental home in their late teens or early twenties for no other reason than to be more independent. It is not, in other words, considered that the parental home continues indefinitely to be the best possible place for young people to live – at least until marriage, or the need to move in search of employment, obliges them to set up a separate establishment. In the case of handicapped young people, by contrast, the parental home continues to be regarded as the optimal environment for them for as long as is humanly possible.

This dual standard is largely attributable to the fact that there are not many satisfactory alternatives to the parental home open to disabled young people who need a good deal of personal assistance. The forms of residential care accommodation which exist are almost exclusively those which, while they offer good physical conditions, are run by the staff as what is euphemistically described as a 'family group' of dependent residents. Such an environment cannot afford a disabled young man or woman any greater independence than could be had in the parental home – if as much. Give the prevalence of this type of residential care provision, it may be correct to assume that, in default of anything more suitable, the parental home is at present the best place for a handicapped young adult to live. This, however, should not seduce us into thinking that no better alternative could or should be envisaged and planned. To persist in regarding the family home as the best and most appropriate setting for disabled young people for as long as the parents can manage to give the necessary care not only imposes a never-ending burden of responsibility and work on the parents (with little, if any, supporting help) but also limits the contacts and experience of the handicapped individual, impeding maturation and keeping him or her permanently rather less than fully adult.

There has been some hopeful development in the sphere of alternatives to traditional residential care in recent years. A number of schemes have started in various parts of the country to provide personal care attendance to disabled people living in their own homes. These schemes open up possibilities for young handicapped people to move out of the parental home into specially designed or adapted flats, houses, or bed-sitting rooms, where their personal care needs could be met by some combination of warden assistance, care attendant scheme, home help service and community nursing service. So far such developments are few and are mostly in the experimental stage – a converted house in the Midlands, a scheme to use Housing Corporation funds to buy a property for four disabled young people to share in a South Coast town, and some specially designed flats scattered throughout the country. Only a handful of disabled young people are at present afforded the opportunity to leave their parental homes for this sort of accommodation, where they can experience the difficulties and satisfactions of living in an independent household in much the same way as their able-bodied counterparts.

Social policy has neglected this area of need among disabled young people. It has been easy to do so because neither handicapped teenagers nor their families have been vociferous in voicing demands for alternatives to living at home, probably because the only alternatives they were aware of were unattractive forms of residential care. The experiences of a young person who is severely handicapped from birth or early childhood are often so restricted that his or her expectations become limited. The parents, who have had to build their whole lives and activities around caring for their disabled son or daughter, have also been restricted in their opportunities and activities. They often become so exhausted and consumed by their responsibilities that their expectations in life are reduced to the one goal of continuing to give the care that their handicapped child requires.

There is, however, one group of disabled young adults whose expectations and relationships with their parents are very much the same as their able-bodied counterparts. These are the young men and women disabled by accidents or injury. The growing toll of road traffic accidents, among the victims of which young adults are over-represented, coupled with advances in medicine which have increased the survival chances of even very severely injured people, means that each year there are more permanently disabled survivors of accidents to swell the numbers of those surviving from previous years.

It is from this group of disabled people, who grew up as able-bodied children and embarked upon adult life with all the normal expectations of independence, employment, marriage, travel, and so on, that the most articulate and pressing demands are heard. Disability at the threshhold of their adult life robs them of many activities and pleasures they once enjoyed or reasonably anticipated. Their functional limitations are, without further considerable and as yet unanticipated medical developments, irremediable, and most of these young people show astonishing resilience in accepting this unpalatable fact. But other limitations; due to social attitudes, lack of provision, or an unaccommodating man-made environment, are fiercely resisted and resented in a way that is far less common among congenitally disabled people brought up from birth with the limited expectations imposed by a handicapped existence. It is not surprising, therefore, to find accidentally disabled people disproportionately represented among the pioneers in new accommodation forms, away from the parental home, for disabled young adults.

Pressure from recently disabled young adults may have played a part in stimulating the development of local schemes of housing and personal assistance. Not only are they often articulate and determined young people who wish to salvage as much as possible of their pre-accident life style, but they are also often in a position to make the telling point that a policy of providing them with homes where they could be largely independent would be cheaper than institutional care. They, unlike the congenitally disabled, can emphasize this point, since the accident from which their disablement arose has often occurred after they had left their parental homes and will inevitably have meant admission to hospital, most probably for very prolonged periods. The cost of special housing schemes for them compares favourably with the cost of a hospital bed indefinitely, or a place in a traditional residential care unit. In the case of congenitally handicapped teenagers living at home at very little cost to public funds, the provision of independent accommodation with some care service would represent an increase, not a saving, in public spending. Their claims can be argued only in terms of improvements in the quality of life available to them, which is a much harder case to make and win in competition with other claims on the public purse.

HELP FOR FAMILIES WITH HANDICAPPED CHILDREN

There are three main areas, other than education and services for teenagers, which have already been discussed, where families with handicapped children might be expected to need help – emotional adjustment to having a handicapped child, practical assistance in managing the disability, and financial provision.

The birth of a handicapped child, as can readily be understood, causes great emotional distress to the parents. There seems to be considerable diversity in the ways parents cope with their distress and reconstruct their views of their handicapped child and their parental role, but whatever their reaction to the situation there is no doubt that all such parents could benefit from emotional support, especially in the early period after the birth of a handicapped baby.[7] In practice, the amount of help of this kind which is received is in most cases extremely slight. The main responsibility for offering counselling or helping parents to work through their emotions seems to be left with the health visitor, but her training does not include anything more than a very superficial introduction to types of handicap to be found in children. Her skills are not basically those of a counsellor, but are directed towards health education and offering families with normal children constructive advice on their care and development. There are now a few courses on handicap available to practising health visitors but it will be several years, at best, before we can expect to have enough health visitors who have been suitably trained to offer the sort of support needed by parents with a handicapped infant. Even then, the health visitor will only be able to give real help if her case load is reduced to permit the time-consuming intensive work with such families which might often be necessary.

As far as practical assistance in caring for a handicapped child is concerned, the health visitor again is the person expected to help the mother to follow the techniques of care which are medically required for her child. Health visitors are generally well equipped to give this sort of practical advice, but specialist techniques of care are, even in cases of very severe handicap, only a minor part of the twenty-four-hour-a-day care which is required. It has become more widely recognized that the more handicapped a child is, mentally or physically, the more he needs and can benefit from the extra stimulation and experience of attending nursery school from the age of two onwards. The mother also benefits from a few hours respite from the demands of caring for her handicapped child. Unfortunately the development of nursery education and pre-school play groups has been slow and came to a virtual halt in the recession of 1980. A large number of families continue to cope with their handicapped children without the assistance which could be afforded by a nursery group placement.

Some, but not all, of the personal care attendance schemes mentioned above give help to families with handicapped children, supplying a competent person to look after the child in his own home for a few hours, or a day, to free the mother. Once again, however, the majority of families in which there is a handicapped child do not live in areas where care attendant schemes operate, and will have access to no organized system of relief care, even in an emergency such as the illness of the mother. In many cases, if grandparents are not available nearby, parents of disabled children even find it difficult to obtain the services of someone in whom they can have confidence to baby-sit while they have an evening out together. Neighbours, who might otherwise offer reciprocal baby-sitting arrangements, are often unwilling to take on what seems to them the rather onerous responsibility of sitting with even a sleeping handicapped child. The very parents who most need a break, and the chance to cement their marital relationship to withstand the strains imposed by having a handicapped child, are the ones most likely to find it difficult or impossible to organize baby-sitting arrangements.

Other forms of practical assistance, such as a laundry service for handicapped and incontinent older children, or local authority help with arranging a holiday placement for the disabled child to allow the parents to go away together, are unevenly available, depending on the provisions made in the local authority area in which the family happens to live. Overall, however, there is little practical relief or assistance available to parents coping with a handicapped child at home.

Apart from the extra physical demands for care which a disabled child inevitably makes on the parents, especially the mother, there are financial costs attaching to any appreciable degree of disability. In every such case some additional expense is likely to be incurred – such as extra laundry charges, special diet, frequent replacement of damaged clothing or utensils, extra heating, special equipment, more frequent redecoration, or being unable to shop economically or use public transport. Yet, despite the extra expense, a family with a handicapped child is less likely than most to have the benefit of a second income from earnings by the mother[8], since even when her handicapped child starts school she may be unable to make the necessary arrangements for his out of school and holiday care to enable her to take up even part-time employment.

Where a child aged two or over is so severely handicapped as to need a degree of supervision or care far in excess of that required by an ordinary child of the same age, the social security system provides for the payment of an attendance allowance, which was first introduced in 1971 [doc 5]. This is payable at two rates, the higher being for those cases where the disabled person needs frequent or continuous attention or surveillance by both day and night, and the lower rate for those who need such attention either by day or by night. The attendance allowance rates are reviewed annually, together with other pensions and benefits. In 1981, £21.65p was fixed as the higher rate, and £14.45p as the lower rate. The money received under an attendance allowance order is not taxable, nor is it taken into account in assessing any entitlement to supplementary benefit, so that it does represent very real financial assistance to recipients and their families, although even at the higher rate it would not cover more than three or four hours of paid care and attention a week. The Department of Health and Social Security is well aware that the attendance allowance is not in general used to buy care attendance. The name of the allocation is derived from the fact that the need for attendance is the qualifying condition to receive the benefit. What the money received is actually spent on is left to the discretion of the individual beneficiary.

Another financial benefit which may be received by a family with a severely handicapped child is the mobility allowance, introduced in 1975 [doc 6]. Disabled people between the ages of 5 and 65 who are unable or virtually unable to walk are eligible to apply and, if the allowance is granted, they may continue to draw it until aged seventy-five provided there is no improvement in walking ability. The mobility allowance is payable at the same rate (reviewed annually) to all recipients irrespective of other income or supplementary benefit entitlement, but it is taxable. The amount payable in 1981 was £14.50p.

The mobility allowance is expected to be used to promote the outdoor mobility of the recipient, although this is interpreted very broadly and no check is made of the way recipients spend their money. A disabled person who cannot be moved for medical reasons is, however, ineligible for the benefit. In practice, very, very few disabled people of any age have been excluded from benefiting from the allowance on grounds of the medical impossibility of mobility.

In the same year (1975) that the mobility allowance was introduced, an invalid care allowance was also incorporated into the social security system [doc 7]. It is payable to those who forfeit the opportunity to work in order to care for a severely disabled person who is in receipt of an attendance allowance. As mentioned already, mothers of handicapped children are known to be less able to take up paid employment than mothers of non-handicapped children. They are, however, not eligible to receive the invalid care allowance since the qualifying conditions exclude married women living with or supported by their husbands. This means that the majority of families with a handicapped child receive no benefit from the invalid care allowance. In 1981 the value of this allowance was £16.30p, and in addition the recipient would qualify for the normal allowance for dependents.

In addition to the above allowances, which come under the national social security system and are available to disabled people other than children, there is a special fund from which discretionary lump sum payments can be made to help families with children who have severe congenital disabilities. This is the Family Fund, administered by the Joseph Rowntree Memorial Trust and originally established by means of a substantial grant from the government. There is no set list of needs for which the Family Fund will give grants but rather the mother of any handicapped child is invited to apply, stating the particular need for which she seeks assistance. This could be, for example, a washing machine, a special tricycle for the child, or a holiday. Thousands of families have been helped from the Fund, and the pleasure and gratification which these grants confer on the recipients have often doubtless been considerable, but the Fund does not, and was never intended to, give regular or long-term financial support to families with handicapped children.

A few children are disabled as a result of some factor for which a culpable agent can be identified and sued for damages. This is so, for example, in the extremely rare cases of accidental injury to infants while in hospital care. It was also the situation of the so-called 'thalidomide children', where the company marketing the drug thalidomide settled substantial sums on the disabled children born to women who could prove they had taken the drug during pregnancy. Throughout the 1970s a campaign was waged by a small group of parents who claimed that their children had suffered permanent and severe brain damage as a result of whooping cough vaccination. In very young babies whooping cough is a serious and sometimes fatal illness, and considerable health education activity had been devoted by the government to encouraging mothers to accept whooping cough vaccination for their infants. Evidence began to accumulate that this normally easy and entirely beneficial vaccination process could, in rare cases, cause prolonged and severe convulsions in the child, sometimes with resulting irreparable brain damage. Some parents of vaccine-damaged children began to agitate for a system of compensation and, following the Pearson Report in 1978 which examined the whole question of compensation for injury[9], the government introduced a scheme to make lump sum payments of £10,000 to any person who could establish that he or she had suffered permanent and very severe damage as a result of vaccination performed under a routine public policy vaccination process.

This is a welcome expression of collective responsibility and concern for the tragic victims of vaccine damage, but the vast majority of handicapped children cannot attribute their disabilities to any culpable agent and are ineligible for any form of compensation. Those most severely afflicted will qualify for an attendance allowance and, if their disability is such as to prevent them walking, also for a mobility allowance. The two together make a valuable contribution to the income of a family which receives them. It must be emphasized, however, that many children with an appreciable degree of handicap are awarded neither allowance, and many severely mentally handicapped children, who may qualify for an attendance allowance, may be denied a mobility allowance because they are physically capable of walking even if they lack the ability to understand requests to walk or to conduct themselves appropriately on public transport, thus making themselves effectively immobile. The wording of the mobility allowance regulations in respect of this point remains ambiguous [doc 8] although Alf Morris, who was Minister for the Disabled at the time the mobility allowance was introduced, has argued that he always intended it should go to both those who would walk if they could, but they cannot; and to those who could walk if they would, but they will not.

Help for families with handicapped children is, therefore, very sparse as far as emotional support is concerned, slightly better but still very inadequate in respect of practical assistance, and reasonably satisfactory for some, but ungenerous to others, in the case of financial provision.

The rather patchy and uncoordinated help given to parents of handicapped children was noted in 1976 in the Court Report on child health services[10] and the recommendation made was that teams of handicap experts should be established in each health district to serve as a source of expertise and advice for the professions involved in the assessment, management and development of handicapped children. Since then, several District Handicap Teams have emerged in various health districts but in a number of cases the co-ordination of health expertise which they have facilitated has been mainly directed towards improving, as a matter of urgency, the situation of disabled adults, who are many times more numerous than disabled children. It is to be hoped that the needs of the latter will not be overlooked in the more pressing concern for the plight of disabled adults.

NOTES AND REFERENCES

1. See, for example, *The Handicapped School Leaver*, BRITISH

COUNCIL FOR REHABILITATION OF THE DISABLED, London (1964); and L. TUCKEY, J. PARFITT AND B. TUCKEY, *Handicapped School Leavers: their Further Education, Training and Employment*, National Children's Bureau, 1973.

2. *Special Educational Needs*, Report of the Committee of Inquiry into the Education of Handicapped Children and Young People, Cmnd 7212, HMSO, London (1976). (Chairman: Mrs Mary Warnock.)
3. See reports of the National Bureau for Handicapped Students, London.
4. Report of the Assistant Adviser on Disabled Students, Open University, published in *Association of Disabled Professionals Newsletter*, 73 Pound Road, Banstead, Surrey, July 1960.
5. P. MITTLER, *People not Patients*, Methuen, London (1976), p. 106.
6. *Ibid.*, p. 108.
7. D. THOMAS, *The Social Psychology of Childhood Disability*, Methuen, London (1978).
8. See, for example, E. M. ANDERSON, *The Disabled Schoolchild*, Methuen, London (1973); and S. HEWETT, *The Family and the Handicapped Child*, Allen & Unwin, London (1970).
9 Royal Commission on Civil Liability and Compensation for Personal Injury, Cmnd 7054, HMSO (1978). (Chairman: Lord Pearson.)
10. DHSS, *Fit for the Future, Report of the Committee on Child Health Services*, Cmnd 6684, HMSO, London (1976). (Chairman: Professor Court.)

Chapter four

HANDICAPPED IN FINDING AND KEEPING EMPLOYMENT

The significance of being handicapped in matters of employment has already been noted when considering the way in which provisions for disabled people tend to be organized along the lines of the three categories of handicapped children, adults of working age, and retired persons.

The ability to work in order to support oneself has always been crucial, and in societies near subsistence level the working population involves practically everyone except for helpless infants and the dying, old and sick – such societies simply do not have enough surplus to support more than a handful of non-productive members. In more technologically advanced societies, with considerable surplus over subsistence, a greater proportion of non-productive members is tolerable. Children and young people are excluded from the workforce in order to be educated for more effective employment roles in adult life, and elderly people who begin to lose the agility of mind and body necessary to embrace new ideas and changing procedures and tasks are thought to be better retired and replaced by younger, more productive workers.

The proportion of the population in advanced societies which is defined as of working age is, therefore, smaller than in simple societies but, for this smaller percentage, work is probably a more significant activity than ever. In social terms, the output of their labour represents the real wealth and security of the society and the basic source of its stability and strength. In personal terms, not only does an individual's work provide his livelihood but it is also the main determinant of his status in society and thus of his esteem in the eyes of the community, his family and himself. To be of working age but handicapped in finding and keeping employment is not just a threat to a person's income, but also to his status.

DISABLED PEOPLE IN OPEN EMPLOYMENT

We cannot know how many people whose disabilities are a handicap to them in the field of employment none the less succeed in finding and keeping a job without any help from official sources, since these people will simply be part of the ordinary labour force and there is no separate record of them. We have no satisfactory estimate of the total number of people in the labour force who are substantially handicapped and therefore we can have only patchy and very partial information about how disabled people fare in the sphere of employment.

The survey carried out by the Office of Population Censuses and Surveys and published in 1971[1] estimated the numbers of people in the population who were impaired in some way and the proportion which was handicapped in matters of self-care. Almost without exception, people judged to be handicapped as far as daily living activities are concerned will also be handicapped in employment. The reverse, however, is not necessarily true, and there are likely to be many more people whose impairments handicap them substantially in finding and keeping employment than would figure in the estimate of the handicapped population made from the survey mentioned above.

For example, the survey estimated there were about 700,000 impaired men and women of working age in Great Britain, but found less than 200,000 to be handicapped. The employment services, however, have the names of half a million people on their register as being handicapped in finding and keeping employment, and believe that only about one-third of those eligible to register in fact do so. This would suggest that there are a million and a half disabled people in the workforce, most of whom never contact or use the employment services for disabled people. Their difficulties and their successes in the employment field can only be guessed at.

QUOTA SCHEMES

The importance of work has been recognized in social policy for disabled people and was the subject of some of the earliest provisions in respect of disablement. In 1919, immediately after the end of the First World War, the government established training centres in which disabled ex-servicemen could be taught new skills to improve their employability, and a scheme to encourage firms to employ them. Those firms which recruited a quota of their labour force from disabled ex-servicemen registered for employment were given priority in the award of government contracts. In 1920 this quota scheme was extended to include civilian blind. The severe recession with high unemployment which affected Britain in the late 1920s and the 1930s largely nullified any beneficial effects which the quota scheme may have had. Not until 1941, with Britain involved in a new war and short of labour for the war industries, did appreciably disabled people have much chance of obtaining employment.

In the spate of social legislation which marked the end of the Second World War, attention was again paid to the employment needs of disabled people. The Second World War, more than the First, had involved a considerable number of civilian casualties, principally from air raids. No longer was the concern solely with disabled ex-servicemen, although their welfare and needs were of great emotional and political appeal in a nation grateful to them for victory and received special emphasis in the provisions which were made for disabled people, particularly in respect of pension arrangements.

The Disabled Persons (Employment) Act 1944 embraced in one comprehensive measure provision to help all adults of working age registered for employment who were substantially handicapped by mental or physical disability in finding and keeping employment. The Act provided for assessment services, courses in rehabilitation centres, vocational retraining and the help of a specialized employment officer – a disablement resettlement officer – in finding work. Maintenance grants were available for those attending courses, whether of a few weeks in a rehabilitation centre or several months for retraining. The Act also provided for employment offices to keep a special register of disabled applicants for work and to issue those who were registered with a green card identifying him or her as a disabled person. The register thus compiled became the basis for a new quota scheme whereby every employer of at least twenty people was required to recruit 3 per cent of his workforce from green card holders, unless granted special exemption from the need to comply with the regulation [doc 4].

There was a period of time after the passing of the 1944 Act when employers were very conscious of the 3 per cent quota obligation. Sometimes this concern took the form of an employer pressuring to register for the green card any employee he already had working for him who happened to have some impairment, although this may have been of no significance in the individual's employment until then. This practice, of course, merely swelled the numbers of green card holders while doing nothing to improve the employment opportunities of disabled people experiencing difficulty in getting work. There were also complaints that holding a green card while in employment actually militated against the chances of promotion for the holder, and in 1958 amending legislation was passed to enable green card holders to withdraw their names from the employment register at any time rather than having to wait, as before, until the time for renewing their registration came round.

In more recent years the value of the quota scheme has increasingly been questioned.[2] The requirements have not been complied with by large numbers of employers and the enthusiasm of disabled people to register has decreased. The latter is probably a consequence, at least in part, of the former, since the advantages of registering are small if employers are not going to observe the quota scheme. Unemployment among registered disabled people is higher than among the general population, and was so even in times of relatively full employment. During recessions it does not appear that being registered as disabled offers a handicapped person any better employment opportunities than he would be likely to have without holding a green card. Of course, as disabled people become less enthusiastic about registering it is likely to be only those having most difficulty in finding employment who will finally agree to register. The concentration among green card holders of disabled people who are hard to place in employment further depresses the readiness of employers to fill their quota, thus reducing still more the success rate of registered disabled people in finding work and leading in turn to greater reluctance to register. By now, there are too few names on the register for every employer to fill his 3 per cent quota even if he wished to do so.

A rather more successful job introduction scheme was launched in 1977, whereby an employer willing to give a chance to a person registered as disabled could take him on for a trial period of six weeks, during which time the employer received a subsidy (£40 a week in 1981) from the Manpower Services Commission. At the end of the trial period the employer could discontinue the disabled person's employment if the experiment had not been a success, or take him fully on to the payroll in the ordinary way. Eighty per cent of the disabled workers placed in employment during the first year of this job introduction scheme were retained at the expiration of the trial period. Unfortunately, despite the success of the scheme, the amount of money available for payments to employers willing to give a disabled worker a chance in this way was cut from nearly half a million pounds in 1979–80 to only £170,000 in 1980–81. Such a sum is only sufficient to assist a thousand disabled people a year to obtain a trial period of employment. This is considerably below the number added to the disabled workforce each year by handicapped school-leavers alone, and in addition there are the even greater numbers of older people who each year become disabled. It is clear that, however great the help which the job introduction scheme affords the few individuals selected to benefit from it, the impact of the scheme on the total numbers of disabled people seeking an opportunity to work is very slight indeed while resources are so limited.

RESETTLEMENT AND RETRAINING FACILITIES

A disabled person, whether registered or not, is entitled to assistance from a disablement resettlement officer. These are people employed by the Manpower Services Commission on the staffs of Employment Service Agencies and specializing in placing disabled applicants in appropriate employment, either in the open market or in sheltered workshops. The officer can also assist a disabled person to obtain a place on a course in an Employment Rehabilitation Centre or a retraining centre, and is able to advise on other facilities offered by the Manpower Services Commission, for example, on how to make use of the Training Opportunities Scheme to undertake further training or courses leading to qualifications for which no instruction is available at training centres. Maintenance grants are available from the Manpower Services Commission for those undergoing training.

Disablement resettlement officers are selected for the work from among Employment Service Agency staff on the basis of suitability and interest and are given a short period of in-service training for specialized work with disabled people. Many of them acquire considerable understanding and expertise in matching disabled applicants to employment opportunities, but few Employment Service Agency employees expect to spend their career in the disablement resettlement branch of the Agency. It is possible that the lack of continuity due to frequent staff changes may be offset by a freshness of approach to employment rehabilitation in the successive disablement officers who each spend a few years in the position.

Courses in Employment Rehabilitation Centres are intended to provide opportunities for a full assessment of a disabled person's potential and difficulties in order to provide practical advice, including adaptations in working position and equipment, to facilitate entry or return to open employment. These courses last only six to eight weeks and do not attempt to impart new skills. For this, a disabled person needs to complete a vocational course at a training centre. He may be placed on such a course after a period of assessment at an Employment Rehabilitation Centre, or he may go direct to vocational training on the recommendation of his disablement resettlement officer.

There are about forty government training centres throughout the country but most of the places at these centres are taken up by able-bodied unemployed people who are being retrained in a more marketable skill. Some disabled individuals will be accepted on courses in these centres, and others will attend vocational training courses at one of the four or five residential training centres which are specially for disabled people. Altogether, something over two thousand disabled individuals a year will receive retraining. For the most part the skills taught at these training centres are manual skills. There are fewer opportunities to acquire non-manual qualifications, although physically impaired people might be expected to have more employment opportunities in the non-manual than the manual field of work.

To some extent the dearth of training facilities in non-manual skills at training centres can be explained by the fact that a disabled person with the inclination and educational background to take up a non-manual occupation can probably follow the necessary training – secretarial, accountancy, administrative, and so on – in the usual centres for further and higher education. Someone who has always been in manual occupations before becoming disabled is not so likely to have the requisite aptitude and educational background for training in non-manual skills, and retraining for a type of manual work which is less exacting than his previous job may be the best compromise.

One cannot be sure that this is the complete explanation of the meagre opportunities for retraining in non-manual skills. One survey of disabled people in 1970 indicated that there were many more who could have benefited from training for non-manual work than were given the opportunity to do so.[3] No marked expansion of training facilities to acquire non-manual skills has taken place since then, so it is quite possible that there are a number of disabled people being retrained for manual employment when they are capable of, would have preferred, and might better have coped with, non-manual work.

It is difficult to get accurate figures of the proportions of all disabled people satisfactorily completing retraining courses who subsequently find and keep employment which utilizes their new skills. One survey of disabled people found that only 15 per cent had received any retraining after disablement, and half of these were subsequently employed in work which did not utilize the skills for which they had trained.[4] The numbers involved in this study were small and the findings may not be typical of the employment experience of retrained disabled people in the country as a whole, but at least it suggests that there is still room for improvement in the retraining and resettlement services for disabled people.

SHELTERED EMPLOYMENT

The employment register which is the basis for the quota scheme also has a second section in which are registered those people judged to be too severely handicapped for open employment, but who might be capable of working satisfactorily in a sheltered environment.

The idea of establishing special workshops in which handicapped people could use their diminished productive capacities dates back to the last century: after the Boer War several workshops for blinded ex-soldiers were established by voluntary charitable funds, the Lord Roberts Workshops for the Blind. The Disabled Persons (Employment) Act 1944 made statutory provision for sheltered work opportunities. The government itself established and ran a chain of more than eighty sheltered workshops, known as Remploy. Local authorities and voluntary organizations, particularly those for the blind, also ran some sheltered workshops and, by the end of the 1970s, something like 14,000 severely handicapped people were in sheltered employment.[5]

Sheltered work facilities are part of the employment services and as such come within the purview of the Manpower Services Commission, even when the workshops are established by voluntary initiative or local authorities. As a form of employment, therefore, sheltered work is paid work, and a disabled person employed in a sheltered workshop draws a wage. He is therefore ineligible to receive a National Insurance Invalidity pension or supplementary benefit, either of which is payable only to those unable to work. On the other hand, as people employed in sheltered workshops are those who have been unable to meet the requirements of the open labour market, they are unlikely to be as productive, even in a specially designed sheltered environment, as a non-disabled worker doing the same job. Sheltered workshops, as part of the employment services rather than a welfare facility, are expected at least to pay their way by producing articles for market at prices and in quantities which will cover the cost of production. Pay in sheltered employment, therefore, although it may be based on the rate for the particular job on the open market, takes account of the lower average productivity of the disabled workers, and earnings are generally low. They cannot be too low, however, if they are to replace the pension or benefit which the disabled person could draw if he were not in employment. Consequently, as mentioned before, any disabled person accepted for employment in a sheltered workshop is expected to be capable of at least one-third of the output of an able-bodied worker. Anything less would reduce the productivity of sheltered workshops to a point where it would cost more money to create the employment opportunities than could be recouped by the sale of the output.

In practice, sheltered workshops do not always cover their costs and considerable government subsidies have been paid. It is arguable that, provided these subsidies do not exceed the amount which would otherwise be paid in pensions and benefits to the people employed in sheltered workshops, there is a net saving of public funds, and the workshops may still be considered cost effective. This is a departure from the normal way of measuring the profitability of a productive enterprise, but it has proved impossible to divorce entirely the welfare aspect of sheltered work from the economic aspect. In so many cases the opportunity to work, even for a wage no higher than the amount which could be received for not working, means so much to a disabled individual that he will seek to obtain or retain a place in a sheltered workshop although his productive capacities may be very low indeed. Those responsible for selecting workers for sheltered employment may find it relatively easy to reject applications from those who, at the outset, are clearly too disabled to be capable of one-third of the output of a normal worker. It is a very different matter to terminate the employment of a worker who is well known and has given good service to a sheltered workshop in the past, but whose condition has degenerated to a point where even his desperate best efforts fall short of the one-third normal output which is demanded.

ECONOMIC VERSUS WELFARE CONSIDERATIONS

The uneasy compromise between economic and welfare considerations in sheltered workshops has persisted from their origins. The Disabled Persons (Employment) Act 1944 acknowledged the importance of the right to work but saw productivity as the criterion for a handicapped person's employability even in sheltered work. In 1957 the employment services for disabled people were reviewed by a Committee of Inquiry appointed by the government under the chairmanship of Lord Piercy. The Committee in its Report[6] expressed general satisfaction with the operation of the employment services for disabled people who could, with help, make a contribution to the economy. The Report recommended only minor changes in provision, and these were incorporated in the Disabled Persons (Employment) Act 1958. Those too severely handicapped to be economically productive were not, in the Committee's view, properly regarded as the responsibility of the employment services, but of the welfare services.

These arguments were recapitulated when sheltered employment was reviewed in 1973,[7] and the logical implication was that not only should the output standard required of employees in sheltered workshops remain as at least one-third the normal output, but also that this standard should be clearly stipulated and rigidly observed. Moreover, the discussion document reminded readers that an important function of sheltered workshops had been seen as the rehabilitation of the employees for open employment [doc 5]. In practice, only an insignificant number of disabled people in sheltered workshops have in the past graduated to open employment. This is not surprising when one considers that the disabled individual who has potential for open employment is more likely to follow a vocational course in a government training centre or, if the skill he possesses is marketable but he lacks confidence or industrial experience, a course in an Employment Rehabilitation Centre. Those disabled people accepted in sheltered workshops are mainly those for whom open employment has been considered and rejected as virtually impossible. If, however, sheltered workshops were to be encouraged to place more emphasis on preparing disabled people for open employment, they would have to be even more selective than at present about the people they accept, and would need to demand a level of capability which offered prospects of open employment eventually. This would inevitably mean that many of the severely disabled people at present employed in sheltered workshops would be denied the opportunity to work.

FINANCIAL INCENTIVE AND DISINCENTIVE AND EMPLOYMENT

It has often been suggested that employment prospects for disabled people could be improved if employers were paid a subsidy for each disabled employee. This argument rests on accepting that a disabled worker is likely to be less productive than an able-bodied worker in the same job, because he works more slowly, because he has more time off sick, or because he needs special equipment or work arrangements which add to output costs. On the other hand, wage agreements increasingly require employers to pay the rate for the job, irrespective of the personal characteristics of the individual employee. Under these circumstances, the argument goes, employers are understandably reluctant to take a chance with a disabled applicant who may well prove to have lower than average productivity. If any employer prepared to consider taking on handicapped workers could be assured of receiving a low productivity supplement for any whose output was markedly below the average for the job, then perhaps a major impediment in the way of employment of disabled people would be removed.

The employment services, however, have always taken the line that to give any sort of subsidy to employers of disabled workers would be likely to create the entirely false and damaging impression that employment opportunities for handicapped people were a matter of charity rather than sound common sense. The official view is that most disabled people can, with minimal assistance, be as productive in an appropriately chosen sphere of employment as any non-disabled person would be. The emphasis of the employment services for disabled people has therefore been on assessment procedures and advice on suitable employment, with some practical assistance in the form of providing aids such as adapted typewriters or special chairs. To offer any continuing subsidy to employers of disabled people has been rejected as only likely to emphasize the inadequacies of handicapped people as workers rather than their potential. Consequently financial assistance to employers of disabled people is limited to the job introduction scheme mentioned above and the possibility of a grant of up to £5,000 from the Manpower Services Commission to an employer prepared to adapt his premises in order to employ a disabled person.

There has been no attempt to free an employer's agreement with a disabled worker from the constraints of any negotiated wage agreement which might be in force. There has been concern lest a disabled person's desire to work might be exploited, forcing him to accept a wage which did not fairly reflect his productive capacity. Not only would this be unacceptable from the disabled person's point of view, but it could also lead to undercutting the able-bodied worker. There is no doubt that many disabled workers maintain a productive level at least equivalent to that of their able-bodied workmates, and the reluctance of the employment services to promote any system which would mean employers paid less for the services to promote any system which would mean employers paid less for the services of a disabled worker than they did for non-disabled people, irrespective of output, is understandable. It does, however, mean that only those handicapped people who can, in the right job, be fully productive, can expect to find employment on the open market. If the employment services for disabled people are expected to promote opportunities for work for people so severely handicapped as to be unable to equal the productivity of able-bodied workers, even with advice and assistance, then the refusal to contemplate any form of subsidy for employers of severely impaired people greatly limits their chances of work. The only real help which is given by the employment services to such seriously incapacitated people is in the form of opportunities for sheltered employment, as discussed above.

Another area where financial considerations have an effect on employment opportunities for disabled people concerns the regulations governing the payment of supplementary benefit or the National Insurance invalidity benefit. Recipients of either of these benefits lose their right to the entire amount of the weekly payment if they take up paid employment. This applies whether or not the employment is full-time or part-time, and even if the earnings from employment are lower than the value of the benefit to which the individual would be entitled if he did not work. The only exception made is when an individual performs a limited amount of work as a therapeutic exercise on the advice of his doctor, when he may earn up to £15 a week without losing benefit. It has been argued that this system discourages a disabled individual from attempting to enter employment unless he is absolutely sure that he will earn, and will be able to continue to earn, a wage substantially higher than the benefit he will forgo. As a worker he will incur travel expenses, liability to pay National Insurance contributions and income tax, and additional costs for meals taken away from home, so that his earnings need to exceed the amount of his benefit quite considerably if he is not to be worse off in work than he would be unemployed. It is true that some financial assistance with travel to work for disabled people unable to use public transport is available from the Manpower Services Commission, but this is normally limited to paying only three-quarters of the total cost of transport, subject to a maximum of £25 per week.

A disabled individual, therefore, must be sure that he can *afford* to go to work before he gives up his supplementary benefit or invalidity benefit to take up employment. Unless a part-time job is really well paid, most disabled people cannot afford to take it, and yet there may be many who are capable of the effort required to work a few hours a day but who could not meet the demands of full employment.

There is a need for a graduated scale of disablement payments which could take account of income derived from earnings. Such a system would remove the obstacles in the way of disabled people taking part-time, occasional, or very low paid employment. It would, however, run counter to a basic principle governing most of our social security system – that payments are made to replace lost earnings. There is a precedent for breaching this principle since the retirement pension, which may be claimed at 65 for a man, or 60 for a woman, is withheld until age 70 for a man, and 65 for a woman, if the individual remains in employment. At later ages the retirement pension is payable in full irrespective of any earnings. In the light of this it is entirely feasible to urge the amendment of regulations to permit disabled people to draw, if necessary on a sliding scale, any invalidity pension to which they were entitled, while at the same time working in paid employment. It is more difficult to envisage such a change being made in the regulations governing supplementary benefit payments but, since the introduction of non-contributory invalidity pensions in 1975, virtually all disabled people eligible for supplementary benefit are also eligible for either a contributory or a non-contributory invalidity pension and would therefore be able to profit from a system which permitted the pension, or part of it, to be paid while the recipient was in employment.

SOCIAL POLICY AND THE WORK ETHIC

As has been pointed out, in many cases disabled people would be no worse off financially if they were unemployed rather than in the low-paid work which is often all that is available to them, if, indeed, they have any employment opportunities. There is no doubt, however, that more disabled people would like to work, even if only in sheltered employment, than are given the chance with existing facilities.[8] The wish to work cannot be, in these cases, primarily a desire for an increased income, since this is often unlikely; nor can it be due to the intrinsic interest of the work as, certainly in sheltered workshops, the tasks performed are often repetitive and unstimulating. Rather it reflects the importance attaching to work as a source of adult worth and status. The disabled person denied the opportunity to work loses self-esteem even when he does not lose any money.

There is some justification for saying that while work as an economic activity is the responsibility of the employment services, occupational activities for those incapable of producing enough to cover the costs of output are a totally different matter and should be regarded as a welfare activity. Attempts by welfare authorities to provide what were called occupational centres have not been successful, however. Some criticisms of these facilities have centred on the unstimulating nature of the occupational activity available, such as basket-making, but the work available in sheltered workshops and even in open employment is, for the majority of workers, boring routine. It is more probable that disabled people attending occupational centres knew that they were not working in the sense that they and the community generally interpret that activity. In other words it is the need to be accepted as having a productive role in society which is important, not so much the money, or the social contacts, or the particular activity involved. And yet such an economically productive role is simply impossible for most very severely handicapped people.

This is perhaps an intractable problem, part of the essence of the tragedy of disablement which social policies may seek to mitigate but cannot entirely eliminate. The problem inheres in the very nature of normal behaviour and values in our society, where work is a central activity in the lives of adults and a basis for our self-esteem and social status. In this atmosphere of the primacy of work, especially for those in the working age-group, to be unable to work due to handicap is not merely a threat to income, which can be made good by a pension; it undermines an individual's whole sense of being a valued member of society.

It is unrealistic to expect employment services for disabled people to operate according to principles contrary to the prevailing work ethic. They have not done so, but they have afforded some help to disabled individuals who needed assistance in entering the open labour market or a rather more protected environment in which to be able to work. They have not helped the very severely disabled or those whose handicap makes it difficult for them to fit into the pattern of present day employment. The social policies of greatest relevance to this group of people are those concerned with income maintenance, and these are discussed in chapter 6.

NOTES AND REFERENCES

1. A. I. HARRIS, *Handicapped and Impaired in Great Britain*, HMSO, London (1971).
2. *Review of the Quota Scheme for the Employment of Disabled People*, Manpower Services Commission, 1981.
3. S. SAINSBURY, *Registered as Disabled*, Occasional Papers in Administration, No. 35, G. Bell & Sons, London (1970).
4. E. TOPLISS, *Survey of Physically Handicapped People under Retirement Age in Private Households in Southampton*, University of Southampton (1978).
5. MANPOWER SERVICES COMMISSION, *Pamphlet EPL 99*, HMSO, (1980)
6. *Report of the Committee of Inquiry on the Rehabilitation, Training and Resettlement of Disabled Persons*, Cmnd. 9883, Vol. xiv (1957). (Chairman: Lord Piercy.)
7. *Sheltered Employment*, a consultative document issued by the Department of Employment, London (1973).
8. J. R. BUCKLE, *Work and Housing of Impaired Persons in Great Britain*, Office of Population Censuses and Surveys, HMSO, London (1971).

Chapter five

ELDERLY AND DISABLED

Two-thirds of all disabled people in this country are over retirement age, and the great majority of these are disabled as the result of degenerative conditions associated with ageing. Many are widowed or single women, living alone with no close relatives nearby.[1] Yet this chapter on the provisions made to assist elderly disabled people is one of the shortest in the book. It is far shorter than those concerned with services for children and adults of working age, who together form only about one-third of the disabled population and, moreover, can rely on greater family support than can many of the elderly handicapped people. The brevity of this chapter reflects the fact that, for those over retirement age who are disabled, the relevant provisions are mainly those relating to supporting services for the elderly population as a whole. These have been examined with clarity and detail in a companion volume in this series, to which the student should refer.[2] The elderly person who is disabled is likely to receive priority in the allocation of services and facilities which exist to help those over retirement age, for example sheltered housing provision, the home help service and meals on wheels.

THE ATTENDANCE ALLOWANCE AND THE ELDERLY

The attendance allowance represents the main form of financial assistance, additional to the ordinary retirement pension, available to elderly people who are disabled. It is payable to those who require considerable and repeated personal attention or surveillance by virtue of a disability which has lasted six months or more [doc 6]. The attendance allowance is not taxable and will not be taken into account in assessing eligibility for a supplementary pension, but it cannot be paid while a person is receiving long-term care in a National Health Service bed or being sponsored by the local authority in residential care. It is, however, payable for any periods spent away from institutional care, for example, a holiday spent with friends or relatives, provided eligibility for the allowance has been previously established and the claim granted, with payment suspended while the beneficiary is being supported by the health service or local authority. It is, therefore, important to establish entitlement to the attendance allowance even when the circumstances of the disabled person are such that it is unlikely to be paid except for occasional periods.

The attendance allowance can be drawn by disabled persons who are supporting themselves in a private bed, a nursing home, or a rest home, and this can be a considerable help in meeting the fees. On the whole, the fact that an elderly person needs to be in an institutional setting in order to receive adequate care is a good indication that a claim for the attendance allowance will be admitted, at least at the lower rate.

A severely disabled person living alone is also eligible to claim the attendance allowance as, although in order to qualify an individual must establish a need for regular and considerable personal attention in matters of basic self-care, the claimant is not required to show that he or she is receiving it from someone resident in the same household or, indeed, from any particular source.

INVALID CARE ALLOWANCE

The invalid care allowance, which is payable to anyone of working age (other than a married woman living with or supported by her husband) who gives up work to care for a person who is in receipt of an attendance allowance, is of assistance in the case of some elderly people. In a majority of cases where an elderly person is disabled, the person most often involved in giving care is the equally elderly spouse. Wives cannot qualify, and husbands who are themselves over retirement age are also ineligible for the invalid care allowance. Daughters are the second main source of assistance to disabled elderly people, and the majority of these are likely to be married and thus unable to claim the allowance. In practice, therefore, the invalid care allowance is of benefit to only a few of the many families caring for a disabled elderly person, but it can be very helpful to the single man or woman, or the divorced or widowed woman, who gives up work to care for a handicapped person. Not only was it worth £16.30p per week in

1981, with additional allowances for dependents, but it also permits the recipient to be credited with full National Insurance contributions, thus preserving pension rights. Supplementary benefit may also be claimed by a person receiving the invalid care allowance if needed to bring his or her income up to the basic standard.

INVALIDITY ALLOWANCE

A person who becomes too disabled to work when still five years or more from the normal retirement age receives an invalidity allowance in addition to any National Insurance invalidity pension to which he or she is entitled. On reaching retirement age the invalidity pension is replaced by the retirement pension, but any invalidity allowance to which the person was entitled continues to be paid in addition to the retirement pension. As the invalidity allowance was only introduced in 1971, no one who was then under 40 years of age and eligible for the highest rate of invalidity allowance has yet reached retirement age. At present, therefore, most of the elderly people in receipt of invalidity allowance will be those who became disabled for work between the ages of 50 and 60 (55 for women), and are drawing the lowest rate of the allowance, which was £1.75p a week in 1981. In the next few years there will be increasing numbers of disabled people reaching retirement age who have qualified for the middle rate of the allowance (£3.45p) payable to those becoming disabled for work when over 40 but under 50, and not until 1991 will there be retirement pensioners drawing the highest rate, currently £5.45p a week, having been disabled for work since before the age of 40.

The majority of retirement pensioners at present drawing an invalidity allowance will be men, since among older women there are fewer who have worked and paid full National Insurance contributions to qualify them for an invalidity pension without which an invalidity allowance is not awarded. Until recently, most married women who returned to employment – a practice which has become increasingly common since the Second World War – elected to pay only reduced contributions covering industrial injury, and were therefore ineligible for most National Insurance benefits, including the invalidity pension. The option of paying reduced contributions is now being phased out, but for some time to come most disabled women reaching retirement age will not have had a contribution record which entitled them to an invalidity pension, and will not therefore be in receipt of an invalidity allowance.

The transference from an invalidity pension to a retirement pension may bring a slight increase in income, as the retirement pension is slightly higher than the invalidity pension and the value of any invalidity allowance payable is also increased by a few pence on retirement. On the other hand, retirement benefit is taxable while, at least for the present, invalidity benefit is not. Those disabled pensioners not liable to pay tax should experience a small increase in income on retirement – a time when their need for comfort, help and support is likely to be increasing.

MOBILITY ALLOWANCE AND ELDERLY PEOPLE

The mobility allowance was introduced in 1975 for disabled people unable to walk. It is payable in full even when the beneficiary is in hospital or being supported from public funds in residential care, and in 1981 was worth £14.50p per week. It cannot, however, be claimed by persons over the age of 65, no matter how incapacitated for walking they may be. Those already in receipt of a mobility allowance when reaching the age of 65 are, under present regulations, permitted to continue drawing it until their seventy-fifth birthday.

As the mobility allowance was phased in gradually, starting with younger disabled people and only extended to the 60–64 age group in 1979, no recipient has yet reached his or her seventy-fifth birthday to be deprived of what is an appreciable supplement to an elderly disabled person's income. When, or if, in future years this does happen, one will feel considerable sympathy for the elderly handicapped person faced with the loss of a mobility allowance to which he has become accustomed, and at an age of increasing difficulty and dependence. The deprivation will seem especially unfair when some disabled people can continue to draw mobility allowance without any age limit. These are the people who were supplied with a car, invalid tricycle or a private car allowance under the old scheme which existed before the mobility allowance was introduced in 1975. They were given the option, with no fixed period in which to exercise it, of exchanging the facility they possessed for a mobility allowance to be drawn in perpetuity.

The absence of any age limit for drawing the mobility allowance in these cases was agreed because the facility which had been enjoyed had been granted without the specification of any age limit for its retention, and it was felt to be only in accordance with general British traditions to ensure that the recipients should not be worse off under the new regulations than they had been under the old. This was a humane and just approach, but it led to inequitable treatment of the two groups of elderly people now receiving assistance with mobility. In addition, an even larger group of elderly people, equally handicapped in movement, whose disability did not manifest itself until after the age of 65, are ineligible ever to receive a mobility allowance at all, let alone retain it.

Data on the elderly population of Britain shows that the proportion considered to be handicapped rises sharply among those over 75. Without some change in the regulations governing eligibility for the mobility allowance it is inevitable that, by 1990, there will be a tiny minority of privileged disabled people drawing a mobility allowance for life; another group making the painful adjustment to the loss at age 75 of a significant part of their income; and yet a third, much larger group, who never benefited from the allowance at all.

If, however, a mobility allowance is to be payable to all disabled people who are unable, or virtually unable, to walk, irrespective of age, then it becomes vital that we have a clear definition of what constitutes a walking handicap due to disability rather than to the reduction of energy and activity which comes with normal ageing. The current regulations which are meant to clarify the factors to be taken into account in deciding eligibility are based on the assumption that all normal people can walk outdoors without assistance from another person, for a reasonable distance at a reasonable pace without undue discomfort or fatigue [docs 7 and 9]. But what does constitute a reasonable distance and pace for a septuagenarian, or an eighty-year old, or someone of ninety? Is everyone who can no longer walk very far, simply because of age, to be considered as virtually unable to walk? Is every confused elderly person, liable to wander or get lost if not accompanied, to be regarded as unable to walk without the assistance of another person? These are questions to which at present we have no obvious answers.

We do not yet have more than very crude guidelines to distinguish between normal old age and handicapped old age. There are many who argue that old age itself is a handicap, and if this is accepted then it makes sense for social policy for elderly handicapped people to be, in general, no different from that for elderly people as a whole. The attendance allowance for elderly people who need regular and considerable help with certain specific activities of daily living, like going to the lavatory, or eating, has worked well and proved a useful financial supplement for the particularly dependent old person. The attempt to extend to the elderly the other special disability allowance, the mobility allowance, has brought problems, and promises more to come. The distinction between people with a walking handicap who are, and those who are not, above the administratively defined age of retirement can be seen to be irrelevant to the needs of disabled people, but its use has been forced upon us by the absence of any clear distinction between normal and handicapped old age.

SEPARATION OF YOUNGER FROM OLDER DISABLED PEOPLE IN RESIDENTIAL CARE

The mobility allowance provides us with one example of the limitations of the system, reflected in much of our social policy, of categorizing disabled people into children, adults of pre-retirement age, and elderly people. Another area where the inappropriateness of this categorization has become obvious is that of residential care.

Under section 21 of Part III of the National Assistance Act 1948 [doc 12] local authorities are charged with the responsibility of providing residential accommodation for homeless families and for those unable to live independently due to frailty, age or disability. As the vast majority of people for whom the local authorities thus acquired a responsibility were elderly people, many of whom would be extremely frail and often confused, the provision of residential accommodation which was made primarily reflected their needs. The much smaller numbers of younger disabled people who were forced to seek admission to residential care frequently found themselves miserably incarcerated in units which were otherwise wholly or principally involved in caring for very old people.

The plight of these younger disabled adults prompted the development of voluntary initiative to provide residential accommodation more appropriate for their needs. In the late 1960s and the first half of the 1970s, local authorities, too, began belatedly to build special residential units for younger disabled people. Both these and the homes established by voluntary organizations, such as the Leonard Cheshire Homes, tended to have admissions policies which favoured disabled applicants who were in their early adult years. Several imposed age limits for admission as low as 40 years, and many would not entertain applications from disabled people who were nearing 60 years of age. These latter were deemed to be at the administrative boundary which determines when old age begins, and were therefore expected to find accommodation in homes for elderly people.

The distinction between disabled men and women who were under retirement age and those who were over, or even near it, was given considerable emphasis in the Chronically Sick and Disabled Persons Act 1970, which carried a clause concerning the separation of younger from older disabled people in institutional care.

Although entirely well intentioned, this emphasis on the age of retirement had unfortunate effects. A few residential units for younger disabled adults even went as far as transferring their residents as they reached retirement age to homes for the elderly. This was not only a cruel unsettlement of the individual concerned, but also entirely inappropriate, as soon became evident.

In homes for the elderly, the majority are over 80 and quite few are under 70. On the other hand, in residential units for younger disabled adults, three-quarters are over 50. A disabled man or woman of 65 or 70, who is otherwise alert and fit, is clearly likely to find the environment of a home for other disabled adults of middle age much more congenial than a home for very old people who are extremely frail and often confused. Increasingly it has been realized that the administrative divisions into which social policy has tended to categorize the handicapped population have misled us into overlooking the real nature of the requirements of handicapped people. The age of a disabled person in, or seeking, residential care is of only limited significance. The important factor is the type of care he needs.

It is only fair to point out, however, that being categorized as elderly is at times an advantage to a handicapped person. There are, for instance, more sheltered housing units for elderly people than there are similar housing facilities for younger disabled people, even allowing for the very different proportions in each age group needing special housing consideration. A handicapped person over retirement age is more likely to be offered sheltered accommodation as a means of prolonging his independence than is a similarly disabled but younger person.

Despite these grounds for slight optimism as far as social policies to help elderly disabled people are concerned, the general picture of provision for them is one where need considerably outruns the capacity of services. This, of course, is true of services for the handicapped population as a whole, but the elderly disabled as a group appear to be particularly poorly supported. Considerations other than individual need clearly have a very strong influence on the availability and distribution of services. The factors involved in establishing priorities for social support are explored in the final two chapters.

NOTES AND REFERENCES

1. A. I. HARRIS, *Handicapped and Impaired in Great Britain*, HMSO, London (1971).
2. A. TINKER, *The Elderly in Modern Society*, Longman, London (1981).

Part two
MONEY AND ACCOMMODATION

Chapter six
INCOME MAINTENANCE FOR DISABLED PEOPLE

The system of income support for handicapped people is bewilderingly complex. It has been the subject of at least one full-length book, which made a telling argument for restructuring, rationalizing and simplifying the benefit system for handicapped people.[1] There has also for the last five years been an annual publication, running to over fifty closely printed sheets, describing and explaining the income benefits for disabled people,[2] and yet even this formidable catalogue carries a disclaimer saying the list is not exhaustive but represents 'a selection of those benefits to which disabled people are eligible and about which questions are most frequently asked'.[3]

The complexity of the system is due to the fact that it has grown piecemeal, without any overall plan or philosophy of collective responsibility for the welfare of disabled individuals. Indeed, disability as a condition meriting support from public funds is recognized in few of the benefits – much more significant is loss of income. Our social security system has developed primarily as a response to factors, deemed to be beyond an individual's control, which lead to an interruption of earnings. The early Poor Laws represented attempts to specify the circumstances in which a person's lack of earnings were to be regarded as a matter for public assistance, or one for public vilification and pressure to become solvent. Someone who was old, widowed, sick or disabled could be regarded as having lost their earning capacity through no fault of their own, and might therefore be given relief. Both the Poor Law of Queen Elizabeth I and the Poor Law Reform Act of 1834 regarded unemployment of an able-bodied person as a situation of the individual's own making. Such a person was to be persuaded or bullied by harsh treatment and very grudging assistance to find work and a sufficient income for himself. It was not until the

National Insurance Act 1911 that unemployment was regarded as a misfortune rather than a misdemeanour (even today traces of the latter view still linger) and a National Insurance scheme was evolved to provide a cash benefit when earnings were interrupted by unemployment. The same Act also provided sickness benefit, for periods when earnings were interrupted by illness, and pensions for widows and elderly people retired from work. Although, therefore, the 1911 Act showed that society was prepared to regard a number of circumstances causing loss of earnings as ones for which the individual could not be blamed or held responsible, the actual misfortune which attracted public support was the same in all cases – threatened destitution due to loss of income.

The same approach was apparent in the post-Second World War legislation. The main focus of National Insurance and National Assistance (later supplementary benefit) legislation was the relief of destitution. Disability per se, without the threat of destitution, was not the subject of financial provision by the state except in cases where the disablement was due to service with the armed forces or to industrial injury.

In both these cases payments are made in respect of the disablement suffered, irrespective of any other source of income, including earnings. State involvement in compensation for injury received while at work came earlier than state commitment to pensions for disabled ex-servicemen. In 1897 legislation was enacted to give employees the right to claim compensation from employers for injury received while carrying out normal duties of the job, providing the employer could be shown to have been negligent in assuring the safety of the worker. Employers, for their part, were legally obliged to take out insurance policies (rather in the way that vehicle drivers are required to be covered against claims for injury from third parties) to cover them in the event of a claim from an injured employee. Subsequently the state took over entire responsibility for industrial injury as part of the National Insurance provisions.

THE WAR PENSIONS SCHEME

Since the Second World War, servicemen whose disability was the result of, or aggravated by, service duties in either war or peace have been entitled to a disability pension. The amount of pension an individual receives depends on the degree of disablement sustained and on his rank. There is an agreed scale which assesses the degree of disablement resulting from an injury. For example, the loss of a foot is assessed as 30 per cent disablement. Those assessed as being less than 20 per cent disabled are awarded a lump sum payment in respect of their disabilities but no pension. A full 100 per cent disability pension for a private was £44.30p in 1981.

The way the basic service disability pension is calculated makes it clear that it is primarily awarded in recognition of loss of function, not loss of income, although this latter consideration is given some recognition by awarding a higher rate of pension to higher ranks who will have lost higher amounts of service pay. As the service disability pension is payable basically in respect of lost functional ability, it is unaffected by any other income, including earnings, which the recipient may have. Moreover, as it is a form of compensation, not a maintenance pension paid to replace interrupted earnings, it may continue to be drawn in addition to any National Insurance income maintenance benefit to which the recipient may be entitled, such as unemployment benefit, sickness benefit, invalidity pension or retirement pension. The only situation that warrants reduction or withdrawal of the service disablement pension is an improvement in, or full restoration of, functional abilities. A war disablement pension is not taxable.

In addition to the basic service disability pension there are a number of allowances to meet special circumstances or needs, such as a constant attendance allowance (payable at one of four rates, on similar lines to the social security attendance allowance but rather more generous), a comforts allowance and an exceptionally severe disablement allowance (both payable to those qualifying for one of the two higher rates of constant attendance allowance), and an unemployability supplement. A very severely disabled ex-serviceman, unable to work, could qualify for all four of these allowances, which together amount to twice as much as the basic 100 per cent disability pension, to which they would be added. A disabled ex-serviceman receiving less than 100 per cent disability pension, who manages to find employment but in a lower paid job because of his disability, can claim an allowance for a lowered standard of occupation.

The service disability pension is fundamentally a compensation to the individual for disadvantages he has suffered as a result of his service duties. It is not primarily geared to avoiding destitution and therefore continues to be paid irrespective of any other income from any source, including earnings or National Insurance maintenance benefits. On the other hand, the emphasis on compensating the injured individual for losses he has sustained means that the service disability pension takes little account of the disabled ex-serviceman's circumstances, including his family commitments. These needs are given recognition in the allowances that exist. Consequently, although payment of the basic service disability pension is unaffected by any changes in the recipient's circumstances other than full or partial recovery, payment of the dependents' allowances is conditional upon the qualifying circumstances continuing to apply. A disabled ex-serviceman, for example, who found civilian employment but at a later date became unemployed could claim National Insurance unemployment benefit on his contributions record in addition to his service disability pension, but he would not be entitled to dependents' allowances from both the war pensions scheme and the National Insurance scheme. An allowance for dependents is a maintenance payment, and not compensation for injury sustained.

A list of allowances available under the War Pensions scheme is given below:

Additional allowances available under the War Pensions scheme:

1. Unemployability supplement, payable to those whose disability is so severe that they are permanently unable to work. This allowance is increased if the claimant has a wife.
2. Constant attendance allowance, payable to those needing frequent attention and help. It is available at four rates, according to the amount of care needed, and individuals may qualify for the lower rate in respect of needs which would not make them eligible for an ordinary attendance allowance available under social security provisions.
3. Exceptionally severe disablement allowance, which is paid automatically to those receiving one of the two highest rates of constant attendance allowance.
4. Comforts allowance, which is paid automatically at a lower or higher rate to those receiving either an unemployability supplement or a constant attendance allowance, or both.
5. Severe disablement occupational allowance, which is paid automatically to those receiving one of the two highest rates of constant attendance allowance but who are nevertheless in paid employment.
6. Reduced earnings allowance, payable to those who have been

prevented by disability from taking up work of an equivalent standard to that performed prior to disablement. The supplement from this allowance when added to the pension received cannot exceed the 100 per cent rate of disablement pension.

7. Treatment allowance, payable to those who have to stop work for seven days or more in order to receive treatment in respect of their disabilities.
8. Clothing allowance, payable to those whose disabilities (or appliances) cause exceptional wear and tear.
9. Age allowance, payable to those with at least 40 per cent disability who are over retirement age.
10. In addition there are a number of other benefits available to disablement pensioners, such as medical prescriptions, allowances for children's education expenses, financial help with housing adaptations, etc.

INDUSTRIAL INJURIES SCHEME

Legislation making some provision for employees to claim for injury sustained at work reached the statute-book before the War Pensions scheme was formulated, but the present much more comprehensive and entirely government administered industrial injuries scheme dates from the National Insurance Act 1948. By this time the War Pensions scheme was fully developed and it served as a model for the Industrial Injury disablement pension. It is calculated according to the degree of disability on the same scale as used to determine service pensions, and those assessed as less than 20 per cent disabled receive a lump sum payment and no pension. The Industrial Injury scheme provides for a pension for those assessed as 100 per cent disabled at the same rate as that received by a private in the armed forces, £44.30p in 1981. The pension is not taxable.

Benefits under the National Insurance Industrial Injury scheme are not dependent on a contribution record. All employees are covered by the scheme, which provides for an injury benefit to be paid for periods of total incapacity resulting from an industrial accident or disease. If after twenty-eight weeks on injury benefit the individual is still incapacitated, an Industrial Injury disablement pension is payable. As this is payable on the basis of assessing the percentage of functional loss sustained by the individual, the pension continues to be payable even if the recipient subsequently returns to work.

As in the War Pensions scheme, the Industrial Injury scheme includes a range of allowances to meet special circumstances. The allowances are not as extensive in coverage as those for disabled ex-servicemen, as can be seen from the list below, nor are the rates as generous.

Additional allowances available under the Industrial Injury scheme:

1. Unemployability supplement, payable to those who, due to industrial accident or disease, are permanently unable to work or able to earn only a very limited amount each year. There are additions to the supplement for dependents and further small additions according to the age of the individual at the time of disablement. This last is the same as the invalidity allowances payable with the National Insurance invalidity pension.
2. Constant attendance allowance, payable to those needing frequent attention and help. It is available at different rates according to the degree of assistance needed. The normal maximum rate is less than the higher rate of the ordinary attendance allowance available under social security provisions, but individuals may qualify for the Industrial Injury constant attendance allowance in respect of needs which would not make them eligible for even the lower rate of the ordinary attendance allowance.
3. Exceptionally severe disablement allowance, which is paid automatically to those who qualify for a rate of constant attendance allowance above the normal maximum.
4. Special hardship allowance, payable to those who are unable to return to their regular work, or work of an equivalent standard, due to their industrial injury or disease. The broad aim of this allowance is to make up the difference between what an individual earns and what he could have earned (increased to allow for inflation) had he not been industrially disabled. For those receiving only a small percentage disability pension, but with greatly reduced earnings, the special hardship allowance is often worth more than the pension.

THE NATIONAL INSURANCE INVALIDITY BENEFIT

A disablement pension awarded under either the War Pensions scheme or the Industrial Injuries scheme is clearly based on the principle of making some compensation for the degree of injury sustained, and in this respect differs considerably from the income maintenance principle which underlies most social security provision, including the National Insurance invalidity pension.

Provision for an invalidity pension grew directly out of the sickness benefit scheme, originally formulated in the National Insurance Act 1911, extended to cover all employees by the National Insurance Act 1948, and amended in 1971 with the introduction of an invalidity pension for those still incapacitated for work after twenty-eight weeks on sickness benefit.

The National Insurance invalidity pension takes no account of the degree of disablement of the claimant. Provided a person with an adequate contribution record remains incapacitated for employment after his entitlement to sickness benefit comes to an end, he will get an invalidity pension. Until 1979 this was payable at a flat rate to all recipients. Since then, some people becoming disabled may be entitled to an earnings related supplement to their pension, in accordance with the graduated National Insurance contributions payment scheme.

In addition to the basic National Insurance invalidity pension, which was £26.00p in 1981, and any earnings related supplement to which a person may be entitled, there may also be an invalidity allowance of between £5.45p and £1.70p payable according to the age at which disablement began. A person incapacitated for work before the age of 40 receives £5.45p invalidity allowance. Those disabled between 40 and 50 receive £3.45p and those disabled over 50 but at least five years before retirement age (60 for a woman and 65 for a man) get £1.75p.

There are also allowances for dependents, which in 1981 were at the rate of £15.60p for a wife or other dependent adult, plus £7.50p in addition to child benefit of £4.75p for each dependent child (under 16, or under 18 if in full-time education). Invalidity benefit is the term used to cover the total payments made under the National Insurance scheme in respect of disability. It is not taxable (although there are government proposals that it should be in the near future) and those receiving it are normally credited with full National Insurance contributions, thus preserving their entitlement to a retirement pension.

The invalidity pension is replaced by the National Insurance retirement pension when the recipient reaches 65 (60 for a woman) but any invalidity allowance to which the individual is entitled continues to be paid in perpetuity. This is presumably because, whereas the pension is a maintenance payment, the allowance is a token compensation for loss of earning capacity – the younger the person when disabled, the greater the number of earning years he has lost and the higher the allowance. This remains true however long the individual lives and so the allowance continues to be paid. The pension, on the other hand, is paid in recognition of the cessation of earnings. This is also true of the retirement pension. An individual cannot be entitled to both pensions at the same time, since a person too disabled for work cannot retire from work, nor can a person too old for work lose employment due to disablement. Only if the invalidity pension was calculated according to degree of disability, like an industrial injury or service disablement pension, rather than on the basis of substituting for absent earnings, could it logically continue to be drawn alongside a retirement pension.

The transition from invalidity pension to retirement pension (with any invalidity allowance payable in addition) does mean slightly more than a change of name, since the basic rate of the retirement pension is a little higher than the invalidity pension but is taxable. On the other hand, the value of the invalidity allowance payable increases by a small amount on retirement. For a disabled pensioner not liable to tax the transition to retirement pension may mean a small net gain in income.

NON-CONTRIBUTORY INVALIDITY PENSION

Until 1975, persons so disabled from birth or early childhood that they could never work, or could not work long enough to build up a National Insurance contribution record, were unable to receive an invalidity pension. For these people supplementary benefit was available, subject to a means test to ascertain that they had no other adequate source of income. In 1975 the non-contributory invalidity pension was introduced, payable to non-insured men and single women of working age who were unable to work due to disability which had lasted at least twenty–eight weeks (the period during which sickness benefit is payable to insured persons) [doc 10].

The non-contributory invalidity pension is payable at a rate of 60 per cent of the ordinary National Insurance invalidity pension (£16.30p in 1981). There are also the normal allowances for dependents. The total non-contributory benefit is not taxable but it is taken into account, as are most other social security maintenance benefits, in assessing eligibility for supplementary benefit.

As most of the people who qualify for the non-contributory invalidity pension would be eligible for supplementary benefit, it means that the total income of most disabled people drawing the non-contributory invalidity pension is no greater than it would be if totally dependent on supplementary benefit.

Perhaps for this reason, the take-up of the non-contributory invalidity pension was much slower than had been anticipated when it was introduced. There are, however, a number of considerations involved in determining whether, in any particular case, it would be to the advantage of a disabled person to claim a non-contributory invalidity pension, or to remain solely dependent on supplementary benefit. Local social security offices are aware of the complexities of the issues and are normally ready to advise disabled individuals on which would be the most advantageous course in their specific circumstances.

There are, of course, some disabled individuals who benefit in full from the non-contributory invalidity pension. These will be people who have a private income sufficient to make them ineligible for supplementary benefit and so will have no reduction in benefit to offset against the pension. However, only a minority of those who are unable to work and build up a contribution record due to congenital disability or disablement in early childhood will be in possession of a private income.

Another group of disabled people has benefited significantly from the introduction of this pension. These are the severely mentally handicapped adults in mental subnormality hospitals who are entitled to the non-contributory invalidity pension, although it will not be paid in full while the beneficiary is in a National Health Service bed. A reduced pension is, however, payable to them, assuring each individual of a weekly amount of pocket money as of right.

THE HOUSEWIFE'S NON-CONTRIBUTORY INVALIDITY PENSION

Disabled married women of working age living with their husbands or being supported by them, and common law wives, were excluded from those eligible for the non-contributory invalidity pension introduced in 1975, and it was not until two years later that the housewife became eligible for an invalidity pension.

This is not taxable and is payable at the same weekly rate as the non-contributory invalidity pension for men and single women, but the conditions of eligibility are different [doc 11].

Whereas the non-insured disabled man or single woman has only to show enduring incapacity for employment due to disablement, the married woman has in addition to show that her disability also prevents her carrying out normal household duties. This extra criterion was introduced because it was argued that many married women were not in paid employment outside the home, so the fact that a disabled housewife was not working did not necessarily mean that it was on account of her disability.

For the married woman who qualifies for the housewife's non-contributory invalidity pension the money received represents a clear gain which is not offset by any corresponding reduction. It is not taxable, so does not increase either her or her husband's tax liability. Neither is it offset against any equivalent loss of supplementary benefit, since a married woman is ineligible to claim this while living with or supported by her husband.

The cost to the country of introducing the housewife's non-contributory invalidity pension is, therefore, a net cost which cannot be discounted against savings in other areas of public expenditure, unlike the non-contributory invalidity pension for men and single women, where the net cost to the country was quite small due to savings in supplementary benefit payments. The government originally budgeted for about 40,000 housewives' pensions, but the number of claims submitted immediately following the introduction of the benefit soon indicated that this figure was an underestimate.

In 1978, less than a year after the introduction of the housewives' pension, new regulations came into force making a stiffer test of eligibility. Not only did a disabled housewife have to show that there were substantial household duties she could not perform, due to disability, but in future she had also to show that those duties which she was still able to perform were insubstantial [doc 11]. It is difficult not to see this move as one to limit the number of claims more nearly to that for which the government had budgeted, rather than any clarification or rationalization of regulations which had proved unsatisfactory in operation.

The housewife's non-contributory pension is likely to be of declining significance since the need for it arises chiefly from the fact that although many married women are in paid employment, they have until recently been able to opt out of paying full National Insurance contributions. This has meant they were ineligible for benefits which rested on a contribution qualification, such as a retirement pension in their own right (rather than a dependent's allowance on the husband's pension), unemployment pay, and sickness and disablement benefits. The option not to pay full contributions is no longer available so that any married women who become disabled in the future may be expected to have a sufficient contribution record to qualify for a National Insurance invalidity pension. If, however, the trend towards increasing employment of married women is reversed, for any reason, then there will continue to be large numbers of married women without an adequate National Insurance contribution record, and for them the non-contributory benefit will still be the only financial help available if disabled while of working age.

SUPPLEMENTARY BENEFIT

The supplementary benefit scheme is primarily concerned not with the financial support of disabled people but with relieving destitution in individuals who have no other means of adequate support. Anyone over the age of 16 living in the community in Great Britain who is not in employment or full-time education has a right to supplementary benefit if his or her income does not reach a specified amount. In the case of a married woman, she is deemed to be supported by her husband either from his earnings or by means of a wife's allowance added to any benefit he receives. She is not, therefore, eligible to apply for supplementary benefit.

Nonetheless, although not designed primarily for the support of disabled people, many of them are dependent on supplementary benefit, although fewer of them are solely dependent on supplementary benefit since the introduction of the non-contributory invalidity pension in 1975. The basic supplementary benefit for a single person is lower than the National Insurance invalidity pension payable to a single individual. The difference in 1981 was about £12 a week. After one year on supplementary benefit, however, the recipient qualifies for a long-term rate of benefit which gives him an income a few pence above that of the invalidity pension. In addition, the person on supplementary benefit will receive a rent allowance which is normally the actual amount of rent paid. He may also qualify for any number of extra allowances known as exceptional circumstances additions, payable to meet essential expenses occasioned by particular needs – such as a need for extra heating or a special diet. These extra payments are small, but an additional one or two pounds can be a significant help to those on low incomes. The supplementary benefit officers also have discretion to make lump sum payments to those on supplementary benefit to meet a special need, such as the purchase of a bed, for example. These grants are known as exceptional needs payments, and anyone drawing supplementary benefit, who believes he has an exceptional need which it is essential to meet is entitled to apply.

In calculating the individual's eligibility to receive supplementary benefit, account is taken of his resources in the form of capital and other benefits, and income, but the attendance allowance and mobility allowance are disregarded entirely. Employment, whatever the rate of pay, makes a person ineligible for supplementary benefit. The only exception is that small earnings derived from work undertaken as therapy, are disregarded. In assessing an individual's capital, any house he or his wife owns in which he lives is ignored, and only other capital above £2,000 (in 1981) affects entitlement. An individual with more capital than this is not eligible to claim supplementary benefit at all under the terms of the Social Security Act 1980. Previously, individuals with capital slightly above the limit were able to draw supplementary benefit at a reduced rate calculated on the assumption that his excess capital was invested and bringing a return of 24 per cent. Even this ungenerous sliding scale has now been abolished.

In theory the supplementary benefit system will provide basic financial support to any individual not in employment whose income falls below the minimum level determined by the state as necessary to sustain decent existence. In addition the officers have considerable discretion to assist individuals with payments to meet special needs. With such an open ended commitment, supplementary benefit could become a really big item in the national budget, demanding in turn ever higher taxation on the rest of the population in order to finance the scheme. The alternative is for the officers to exercise great vigilance in order to ensure that any payments made are the minimum necessary to avoid utter destitution. In general the emphasis has been towards the latter alternative. All applicants for assistance are subjected to a searching means test. Benefit, except for unsupported mothers of young children, persons over retirement age, and those identified by a doctor's statement as disabled, is conditional upon registering for employment, thus demonstrating an intention of becoming self-supporting as soon as possible. Where there is discretion as to whether to give support or not, or over the amount of money to give, as, for example, in making exceptional circumstances additions or exceptional needs payments, officers tend to err on the side of parsimony rather than indulgence.

The blame for this, if blame is appropriate, does not lie with the officers, since their actions are constrained by the policies and guidelines imposed by the Department of Health and Social Security and endorsed by the public as a whole in its electoral choices. These constraints are such as to require the officers to account for every penny of expenditure, which must be justified as absolutely necessary to assist people in real need. They are subject to criticism for any money wasted on 'scroungers' who have, or could be deemed to be capable of getting, other means of support. On the other hand, the officers are never required to justify failure to give assistance to all those who are eligible but fail to claim due to lack of knowledge or reluctance to submit to a searching and, to them, humiliating examination of whether or not their need is genuine. Consequently, although in theory the supplementary benefit system offers a humane and infinitely flexible scheme of financial assistance to meet needs in diverse human situations, in practice recipients are often critical of the ungenerous and unsympathetic way in which their needs have been assessed.

OTHER FINANCIAL ALLOWANCES IN RESPECT OF DISABILITY

In addition to the various pensions and supplementary benefit provisions which have been described above, the British social security system includes three special allowances in respect of disability – the attendance allowance, the mobility allowance, and the invalid care allowance.

These have all been described in Chapter 3 in connection with provision for families with handicapped children. The information given in respect of the attendance allowance and the invalid care allowance applies irrespective of the age of the disabled person concerned and therefore need not be repeated here. In the case of the mobility allowance, the age of the disabled individual can be of considerable significance. The way in which this allowance relates to elderly people has been described in Chapter 5. Here we are concerned with a scheme connected with the mobility allowance.

Motability is a scheme to assist holders of the mobility allowance to obtain a car. It is run by a voluntary organization but was developed in response to government initiative, with considerable financial help from the government at the beginning. It operates both car lease and car hire purchase schemes. The car lease scheme provides a car in return for the disabled person's mobility allowance for three or four years, plus a lump sum in advanced rental payment, which varies in amount from a few hundred pounds to about two thousand pounds according to the make of car supplied. The disabled person is also responsible for paying for any adaptations or alterations to the car which he needs. The car is then maintained by Motability for the duration of the lease, although the disabled person has to meet the cost of petrol – he can, however, claim exemption from payment of Vehicle Excise Duty. At the end of the lease the car reverts to Motability, but the disabled person can take out a lease on a new car, paying the advanced rental sum and the cost of adaptations as before.

The hire purchase scheme also requires the disabled person to pay over his mobility allowance to Motability, in this case for four-and-a-half years, and to pay a lump sum deposit. The amount needed for deposit varies according to the make of car, but is greater than that required in advanced rental for the same model. The disabled person has to pay for any adaptations made to the car and for all maintenance and repairs as well as running costs. At the end of the four-and-a-half years, the disabled person owns the car outright.

The Motability schemes have proved very popular, although the steep inflation which occurred soon after the schemes were introduced forced a sharp rise in the advanced rental payments and deposits required, putting car ownership, even on the favourable terms of Motability, out of reach of many disabled recipients of the mobility allowance.

CONCESSIONS AND GRANTS

There are several financial concessions and grants available to disabled people, some of which have already been mentioned, such as exemption from liability to pay Vehicle Excise Duty, and training grants from the Manpower Services Commission (see Chapter 4). There is also a special allowance from local authorities for disabled students on higher education courses and in receipt of an ordinary local education authority mandatory grant.[4] The amount of special allowance that a student receives depends on the additional extra expenditure he necessarily incurs on his course as a result of his disability. The maximum amount payable in any one year of his course was £235 in 1981. A disabled student not receiving a local education authority grant may be eligible for supplementary benefit. This is a concession, as non-disabled students are not eligible for supplementary benefit during term time, whether or not they hold a grant, as they are not available for employment, which is a condition of receiving benefit. In the case of a severely disabled student, supplementary benefit can be paid if it is accepted that he would be extremely unlikely to find employment even if not a student.

Another concession which benefits a number of disabled people is that, in assessing eligibility for a rent or rate rebate from the local authority, a disabled person is deemed to have special needs and therefore more easily satisfies the conditions for a rebate allowance. Moreover, in calculating a disabled person's income for the purpose of assessing the amount of rent or rate rebate due, no account is taken of money received under attendance allowance or mobility allowance orders, and the first £4 of any disability pension is discounted.

Other grants, such as those to assist with housing adaptations, holidays or telephone installations, will be discussed in Chapter 6, where we examine policies for providing personal social services and practical assistance to handicapped people in their own homes.

NOTES AND REFERENCES

1. J. SIMPKINS, *Whose Benefit?* Disablement Income Group, London (1978).
2. *Disability Rights Handbook*, Disability Alliance, 1 Cambridge Terrace, London N.W.1, published annually.
3. *Disability Rights Handbook 1980*, p. 3.
4. For details of grants, see *Grants to Students – a brief guide*, DEPARTMENT OF EDUCATION AND SCIENCE, London (available free).

Chapter seven
RESIDENTIAL PROVISION

The provision of personal care and practical assistance to disabled people falls into two main divisions, that of residential care and that of support and assistance to disabled people in their own homes. The relevant instruments of policy are the National Health Service Act 1946, the National Assistance Act 1948, the Mental Health Act 1959, and the Chronically Sick and Disabled Persons Act 1970.

When the National Health Service Act 1946 became operative, in July 1948, the Health Service took over all the mental subnormality, geriatric and other long-stay hospitals which had until then been run by the local authorities. Many of these hospitals had originated under the old Poor Law system as workhouse infirmaries or asylums, and had only become local authority responsibilities when the provisions and services under the Poor Law had been transferred to them in 1929. Immediately following that transfer of responsibility the country suffered a major economic recession, from which it was only beginning to recover at the outbreak of the 1939–45 war. Consequently the long-stay hospitals were still very little different when the National Health Service took them over in 1948 from when they had formed part of the Poor Law system. In appearance they were forbidding and depressing, with totally inadequate facilities and staffing. They were places of last resort which people entered involuntarily and unwillingly when all else had failed. Even in 1962, Peter Townsend, writing of institutional care for elderly people, entitled his book 'The Last Refuge'.[1]

While elderly people, many of them disabled, formed a major part of the population of the long-stay hospitals, another large group was composed of severely mentally subnormal people. The mental subnormality hospitals, often with several hundred beds arranged in large bare wards, were the only homes many mentally subnormal individuals ever knew. A fairly common sight forty years ago was a drably uniformed crocodile of mentally defective children being marched through the streets. These were the high grade defectives whom it was deemed safe to bring into public thoroughfares for an exercise walk, to be locked away again afterwards behind the big iron gates that shut the mental hospitals off from society.

For younger physically handicapped people there was no special institutional provision. If they could not be cared for by relatives or friends in their own homes, a bed in a geriatric hospital or a mental subnormality hospital was the most likely outcome in the years before the National Health Service, and is still quite possible today.

The National Assistance Act 1948 made provision for meeting needs that were not covered by other forms of welfare, such as the Health Service or National Insurance. A major part of the Act was concerned with providing financial support to persons with inadequate incomes who were not covered by National Insurance schemes. It had originally been anticipated that these would be mainly elderly people who were too old to be included when the National Insurance pension scheme started. In time this group would disappear and, apart from isolated cases, it was thought that the comprehensive provisions of National Insurance would virtually eliminate the need for National Assistance. This, as we know, did not happen, and the financial benefit aspects of the National Assistance Act were taken over and modified in the Social Security Act 1966, and renamed supplementary benefit.

RESIDENTIAL CARE FOR YOUNGER DISABLED PEOPLE

Part III of the National Assistance Act is the major policy instrument for the provision of residential care for those who are unable to look after themselves by reason of age or infirmity [doc 12]. This is still the basis for local authority responsibility to provide care for disabled individuals who do not need hospital treatment but cannot be cared for in their own homes. According to the Act, local authorities could discharge their obligations to ensure the care of disabled people either by building and running local authority residential units, or by accepting the financial responsibility for the accommodation of their disabled citizens in homes run by voluntary organizations.

In the decade following the National Assistance Act 1948, the major pressure for residential accommodation was from the growing numbers of very old people in society, so that local authorities were fully stretched in trying to expand and improve provision for them. The younger physically disabled person needing residential care was still generally accommodated in a geriatric unit. The main difference was that the unit was increasingly likely to be run by the social services rather than as a geriatric hospital under the National Health Service. The younger mentally handicapped person who could not be kept at home continued to be imprisoned in one of the large locked mental subnormality hospitals.

In order to fill the vacuum, voluntary organizations entered the field of residential care for younger handicapped people. Most of the voluntary effort centred on younger physically disabled adults in need of residential care, but there were a few voluntary homes for mentally handicapped young people, such as those run by the Spastics Society for victims of cerebral palsy who were both mentally and physically defective. Voluntary organizations were able to concentrate on raising the capital cost of a home for disabled people, secure in the knowledge that the running costs could be met wholly or in large part by the fees charged for each resident admitted. Those unable to meet the full cost out of their own resources could be financially assisted by their local authority, under section 21 of the National Insurance Act 1948.

Some disabled residents would be drawing a National Insurance invalidity pension and perhaps an occupational pension as well. For these people the local authority would need to contribute less in order to make up the full fee. Others, for example most congenitally disabled people and severely incapacitated housewives were, until the introduction of non-contributory pensions in the mid-1970s, without any income of their own and the local authority would have had to meet the full cost of their care. None the less, the arrangement was still attractive to local authorities since the fees charged by voluntary organizations rarely reflected the capital cost of the home, which was met by voluntary donations, or the full cost of depreciation. For some years data were published in a form which permitted a comparison to be made between the average cost of care for handicapped people in homes run by voluntary organizations and those run by local authorities.[2] The former were distinctly cheaper, but similar published information is not now available.

Most local authorities were therefore content to allow voluntary organizations to make a significant contribution to the provision of residential care for younger handicapped people and even today almost half the physically disabled adults under retirement age in residential care are accommodated in units run by voluntary organizations. Some local authorities made little use of their permissive powers to establish units of their own for younger disabled adults preferring to use accommodation provided by voluntary bodies. This inevitably meant that provision was unevenly distributed throughout the country, since it reflected the geography of local authority commitment and voluntary initiative and success in fund-raising, rather than the geography of need for care. Moreover public enthusiasm for contributing towards the care of disabled people is not evenly stimulated by all types of disability. In particular, mental handicap seems to arouse less practical sympathy, and voluntary provision of residential care facilities for mentally handicapped people has never equalled the extent of such provision for physically handicapped individuals.

Local authority responsibility for the residential care of mentally handicapped people was given new emphasis by the Mental Health Act 1959. This Act followed the report of a Royal Commission which reviewed the treatment of mental illness and mental deficiency[3] and recommended changes to bring the treatment of mentally disordered and mentally defective people more in line with modern therapeutic techniques. The Mental Health Act 1959 gave statutory expression to the recommendations of the Royal Commission by removing the barriers which had existed to the treatment of psychiatrically ill patients in general hospitals, and by restricting the circumstances in which mentally ill people could be compulsorily admitted to, or detained in, hospital. As far as possible, the mental health services were to be community based rather than hospital based. This meant that local authorities were given a whole new range of responsibilities for day care, social work support and residential care of mentally ill and mentally subnormal people. The powers which were thus conferred on local authorities were, however, permissive not mandatory, and although since 1959 there has been a steady decline in the numbers of patients in mental hospitals, this has not been matched by a corresponding expansion of care facilities in the community.

Following the publication of two official reports, one on services for the mentally ill[4] and the other on services for the mentally handicapped,[5] there was further emphasis on the need for more community care provision, including hostels and residential care units. Further encouragement was given in the government's declaration of priorities for the health and personal social services in 1976.[6] To facilitate the development of community based provision, the government allocated special funds, to be administered by Area Health Authorities but spent only on projects jointly agreed by both the health services and the personal social services. It had, of course, always been open to health and social service agencies to co-operate, and some community projects supported by both and funded by contributions from both budgets already existed and continued to be developed after 1976. The special funds, however, were extra to both the area health service budget and the local authority budget for the personal social services.

These special allocations continued into the 1980s but their effect on the development of additional new services has been slight. Some new services and facilities to benefit handicapped and elderly people were launched but, although financed from the special fund for the first few years, such provisions were expected subsequently to be accepted as a charge on the local authorities' social services budgets. In the economic recession at the end of the 1970s and early 80s, social service budgets were severely curtailed and those of the health services were also restricted. In this situation of threat to the maintenance of existing services, the local authorities were very reluctant to commit themselves to projects for which they would have to accept full financial responsibility in a few years. The joint finance monies were increasingly used, not to mount improved services, but simply to maintain existing facilities, such as supplying aids to handicapped and elderly people, making housing adaptations enabling them to continue living at home, and meeting the cost of care in nursing homes or residential units for handicapped people whose living arrangements had completely broken down.

ECONOMIC RECESSION AND RESIDENTIAL CARE

Such projects for expanding residential care facilities for mentally and physically handicapped people as were embarked on in response to central government encouragement and exhortation in the mid-1970s were largely completed by the end of the decade. There were very few plans for any further developments, due to the cuts in health and welfare expenditure. In the case of physically handicapped people residential facilities were doubtfully adequate. In the case of mentally handicapped people they were still utterly inadequate, and for most of them the alternatives were still living at home with the family and little community support, or a bed in a mental subnormality hospital. Most parents of mentally handicapped children want to keep them at home for as long as possible, often accepting without complaint a burden of unrelieved surveillance and care which severely restricts their own activities, income and contacts.[7] Inevitably the time comes when the parents are too old to cope and are forced to surrender their handicapped son or daughter to institutional care. The dearth of good residential facilities for mentally handicapped people means that many parents struggle on to the point of exhaustion, illness or death, so that for their handicapped child the trauma of moving to a new environment is compounded by the distress of receiving few, if any, visits from aged and ailing parents.

The unsuitability of a hospital-type environment for mentally handicapped people has been repeatedly stressed. The Victorians saw mental deficiency as a threat, like mental illness, from which society must be protected by locking away in huge asylums all those who were mentally subnormal or mentally ill. The Mental Health Act 1959 stressed the greater suitability of community care for mentally handicapped people who were not in need of hospital treatment. The Education Act 1970, which transferred the responsibility for educating and training severely subnormal children from the health services to the education services, emphasized the fact that the appropriate treatment of mental handicap is educational not medical. In 1979 there was the Jay Report on the care of mentally handicapped people,[8] which again stressed that mental subnormality is not a medical or nursing problem and urged a thoroughgoing revision of the type of training given to staff responsible for the care and development of mentally handicapped people.

The Jay Report provoked a good deal of discussion and considerable opposition, especially from nurses in mental subnormality hospitals. They argued, with some justification, that they had trained especially for registration as mental subnormality nurses and were equipped to give appropriate care to mentally handicapped people, but lacked suitable buildings and adequate resources.

After a delay of over two years, the government decided not to accept the main recommendations of the Jay Report and left institutional provision and staffing for the care of mentally handicapped people virtually unchanged, thus perpetuating the problems of the mental subnormality hospitals. Not only were no extra resources allocated to this branch of the hospital service, but from its already deprived position it was left to bear its share in the cuts in public expenditure made after 1979. The prospects for mentally handicapped people who need to live in a residential setting continue to be depressingly bleak in the 1980s.

Physically handicapped adults unable to live in private households have fared rather better than the mentally handicapped as far as residential provision is concerned. This was at first almost entirely attributable to the efforts of voluntary organizations, notably the Leonard Cheshire Foundation, to provide suitable residential accommodation for physically disabled people who needed a lot of personal assistance in order to manage essential living activities, but who were not ill or in need of hospital treatment. Some local authorities subsequently made a contribution to the stock of residential accommodation for physically handicapped adults, particularly in the climate of greater concern for disabled people following the enactment of the Chronically Sick and Disabled Persons Act 1970.

It is interesting to note that where voluntary organizations have been active, as in the field of residential care for younger physically handicapped adults, far from reducing local government involvement, it seems positively to have stimulated it. Where, as in the case of residential provision for mentally handicapped adults, voluntary provision is small, local authority commitment is similarly limited. Voluntary initiative may be seen less as a way of plugging gaps in the statutory services than as a stimulant and pacesetter.

Despite both voluntary and statutory effort on behalf of physically disabled adults, difficulties are often experienced in finding a place in residential care for a severely handicapped adult who can no longer be cared for at home. This is particularly the case if the person seeking admission is middle-aged and heavily dependent as the result of a progressive condition. Yet these are the characteristics of the majority of people at present wanting to enter residential care. Multiple sclerosis, a progressive and disabling disease of the central nervous system with no known cause or cure, accounts for the largest single group of heavily disabled adults under retirement age in residential care. Typically it first becomes apparent when the victim is in his twenties and progresses, often with some periods of spontaneous remission, until the individual is completely helpless. By the time someone with multiple sclerosis becomes so heavily handicapped that the family can no longer manage physically to give the necessary care, the disabled individual is likely to be about fifty. In addition to multiple sclerosis cases, other large groups seeking residential care are those crippled by severe arthritis, and survivors of strokes who have been left very disabled. People with either of these conditions needing residential care are also likely to be in late middle age, or even older.

Relatively few young adults are so disabled, and so isolated from relatives able to give care, that they seek to enter residential units. With unmarried young people this may be due more to the lack of attraction of residential care as at present generally organized than to a positive desire to remain in the parental home, since the normal expectation of young people is to move away from parents. Whatever the reason, the fact remains that young disabled adults form only a small proportion of physically handicapped adults in residential care. For the severely disabled young person who does apply, it is not usually too difficult to find a voluntary organization home or a local authority unit willing to accept him. It is less easy to find a place for a heavily physically handicapped adult of late middle age.

ADMISSIONS POLICIES AND NEED

The early Cheshire Homes were among the first in the field of residential care specially planned for younger disabled, and they were able to fill places mostly with young residents, some of whom thankfully exchanged a bed in a geriatric ward for a place in a Cheshire Home.

The Chronically Sick and Disabled Persons Act 1970 again emphasized the need to separate younger from older handicapped people. Alf Morris, the Member of Parliament who in 1969 drew first place in the annual parliamentary ballot for the opportunity to introduce a Private Member's Bill, announced his intention to frame a measure to improve services for handicapped people and invited suggestions from interested bodies and individuals. In the voluminous mail he received were a number of distressing letters from young disabled people, or from their relatives on their behalf, who had spent years miserably incarcerated in geriatric wards. He therefore included in his measure a requirement that both the Health Service and social services should make annual returns to the Department of Health and Social Security indicating the number of persons under retirement age who were accommodated with persons over sixty-five.

As in most cases the conditions causing disablement are crippling rather than killing disorders, an individual taken into residential care may well live for many more years. Consequently, a person already in his late fifties when admitted might be expected to survive beyond the age of 65, and would then appear in the returns made to the Department of Health and Social Security as an elderly person in residential accommodation, rather than one of the younger disabled population. The emphasis which the Chronically Sick and Disabled Persons Act 1970 placed on the separation of younger from older disabled people made this sort of natural ageing of residents seem undesirable, and reinforced the tendency of units established to care for younger disabled adults to impose quite a low upper age limit for admission in order to delay the time when any resident should reach the age of sixty-five. This policy, however, did not match the real pattern of demand from disabled people for residential care.

It became increasingly evident that, with the expansion of voluntary and statutory residential provision for physically handicapped adults, there would soon be unfilled places unless some applications from middle-aged disabled people were accepted. None the less, preference continued to be given to the young person with a static disability such as the paralysed victim of a road accident. The severely handicapped person over 55, who has struggled against progressive disability to maintain an independent home life as long as possible, is still often dismayed to find that no residential unit has room for him when he finally asks for care.

By 1980, however, the disabled individual of any age who needed a place in residential care was facing a new problem. There was no longer any certainty that, even if a suitable vacancy could be found, the local authority would agree to accept responsibility for meeting the cost of residential care. Few of the severely handicapped people forced to seek admission to residential care have personal incomes sufficiently high to meet in full the weekly charges, which in 1980 averaged about £120 a week in units for younger disabled adults.

Social services budgets were cut after 1979 as part of the government's policy to restrict public expenditure in an effort to curb inflation, and local authorities became extremely cautious about incurring financial responsibility for people entering residential care. Some units run by voluntary organizations found that while any vacant place they had might be eagerly sought by several severely disabled people whose home circumstances were perilously difficult, it was very difficult to get a commitment from the relevant local authority to sponsor any of the applicants until funds were released by the death or discharge of someone else who was already being supported in residential care. An individual's need for residential care was a lesser factor than the availability of funds. Although ability to support oneself in residential care was not envisaged in the National Assistance Act 1948 as a relevant criterion determining admission to care, it had become a prominent consideration by the beginning of the 1980s. The disabled person who had a house to sell and could finance his own residential care out of the proceeds for a few years before the local authority would need to give him financial assistance became a more attractive person for a local authority to sponsor in residential care than someone, possibly even more disabled and needy, who had no such capital and would be a financial cost from the day of admission. If the home circumstances and care arrangements for the latter should completely break down, it would probably result in an emergency admission to hospital at no charge at all to the local authority budget.

Such strategies may well effect some overall savings in public expenditure, since many of those experiencing difficulty in gaining admission to residential care will simply struggle on for a while longer at home, enduring neglect and privation or the distressing awareness of being an intolerable burden to exhausted relatives. Only a minority, albeit perhaps a significant minority, will experience a dramatic disaster, such as a serious fall or the death of a caring relative, which will mean long-term admission to a hospital bed at a cost considerably higher than residential care. The amount of public money saved, and the cost of such economies to disabled people and their families in terms of discomfort and distress, are important and serious issues, but the point to be emphasized here is the way in which local authority responsibility for the welfare of disabled people is interpreted in accordance with the current economic situation. Section 21 of the National Assistance Act 1948 appeared to lay a mandatory obligation on local authorities to provide residential accommodation for disabled people unable to cope in their own homes [doc 12]. Yet when financially inconvenient, the fulfillment of this obligation can apparently be ignored or indefinitely delayed.

This appears to be for two main reasons. First, section 21 does not specify clearly the circumstances which constitute a need for residential care, so the local authorities may vary the standards applied to determine need in accordance with the availability of funds to meet the needs thus identified. Second, any action to compel a local authority to fulfil its obligations under the Act, according to the procedure laid down in the Act, must be taken by the Secretary of State at the Department of Health and Social Security. This is a political appointment and the Secretary of State cannot therefore be expected to use his powers to compel local authorities not to make economies which he, as part of the government of the day, has ordered to be made.

The situation demonstrates yet again the fact that social policies to assist and succour the handicapped population exist within the context of the overall political and economic matrix. They do not stand alone as an expression of humanitarian concern divorced from the materialistic considerations of society. The same message is conveyed by the examination, undertaken in the next chapter, of supporting services for disabled people living in private households, the provision of which was made mandatory for local authorities under section 2 of the Chronically Sick and Disabled Persons Act 1970.

STANDARDS AND STAFFING IN RESIDENTIAL CARE

Establishments other than those run by local authorities or the National Health Service which provide residential accommodation for handicapped people may be registered as nursing homes, or Part III accommodation, or in some cases, both. Under the Nursing Home Act 1975 there is provision for nursing homes run by voluntary organizations or privately for profit to be registered by the health authority in which the facility exists. In order to be registered a nursing home must comply with the standards laid down by the health authority concerned. These are not standard throughout the country but normally cover such matters as the maximum number of beds to be installed in the accommodation, numbers of lavatories and baths, compliance with fire and safety regulations, drug security, and the ratio of state registered nurses to patient numbers.

The Residential Homes Act 1980 provides for the registration by local authorities of premises run by voluntary bodies or private agencies for the purpose of providing residential accommodation for people for whom the local authority has accepted a responsibility under section 21 of Part III of the National Assistance Act 1948; hence the term, Part III accommodation. Local authorities require premises registered as Part III accommodation to comply with standards of physical amenity not dissimilar to those required by health authorities of nursing homes. No stipulation about staffing qualifications is made by local authorities in respect of Part III registration. In several areas of the country it is possible for the same establishment to be registered partly as a nursing home with the health authority and the remainder as Part III accommodation with the local authority, with differing staff requirements for each part of the home although there may be no real difference in the degree of dependence or type of care needed by the residents in the different sections of the home.

The situation is currently under review, but at the time of writing only a registered nursing home can be used by the National Health Service as a place to which a patient can be transferred and paid for out of health service funds. Payments for such people are normally at a higher rate than payments made by a local authority in respect of anyone they sponsor in residential care. The extra payment is in recognition of the fact that those people sponsored by the National Health Service are judged to need constant nursing care, although they do not need hospital care, hence the requirements for trained nursing staff whom it is accepted will be more expensive than untrained staff.

It is doubtful whether disabled people who do not need hospital care may be said to need constant nursing care such that only nursing home care is suitable for them. After all, most severely disabled people live in their own homes where relatives give the care that is needed, with perhaps the regular help of a district nurse. Nor is there an obvious difference between disabled people in nursing home beds and those in Part III accommodation. There seems little justification for assuming, as the registration regulations seem to imply, that where nursing qualifications are not essential, completely untrained care staff will suffice.

This, however, is broadly the picture of staffing in residential units for handicapped people. Only about 2 per cent have any qualifications at all, and the majority of those with a qualification are nurse trained. While recognizing the value of nursing skills in some situations in residential care, and applauding the commitment and humanitarian understanding of many of the nurses concerned, it must be strongly emphasized that the care needed by people in residential units is not primarily or mainly nursing care. On the other hand it is recognized that while relatives of a disabled person might, without any special training, gradually acquire the techniques necessary to give basic personal care and develop sensitive awareness of their loved one's emotional needs, the same is not necessarily true of staff in residential units who are assisting a number of people with different disabilities and different personalities. Such staff need training in the skills of basic personal care and, even more importantly, in understanding the needs and attitudes of disabled people and their own responses to them.

A new form of training, the Certificate of Social Service, has been introduced to meet this need.[9] These courses have expanded rapidly over the few years they have been running. The training is in-service training, normally requiring one day a week at college over a period of three years, plus independent reading and study. With so many completely unqualified people working in the residential care field, some in senior positions, it made sense to develop a form of training which could be taken by those in post. In fact, however, it proved an expensive form of staff training, since in order to free an individual for one day a week in college and the equivalent of another whole day a week for private study, replacement staff had to be engaged. In addition there were the college fees, travel expenses and book requirements of the student. Although, therefore, many local authorities and some voluntary organizations very much welcomed the development of Certificate of Social Service courses, the enthusiasm for funding members of their residential care staff for such training was considerably dampened by the harsh economic climate of 1979.

Very vulnerable disabled people continue to live in residential care units where the staff, if trained at all, are trained only in ways to meet their physical needs, and not in the vitally important matter of understanding their emotional difficulties and needs. A well trained, which means appropriately trained, staff is probably the best guarantee of a good standard of care. This guarantee is singularly lacking in the residential care field. The only standards regularly inspected are those required for registration as a nursing home or Part III accommodation but these, as made plain above, cover only physical amenities. The importance of these is not minimized, but good physical conditions in a residential unit are entirely compatible with a complete lack of personal privacy, a denial of opportunities for independent action, and a very poor quality of life altogether for people in that unit. This point was strongly emphasized in a paper published by the Personal Social Services Council entitled *Residential Care Reviewed*,[10] but no action was taken and the Council itself was disbanded in 1979 as part of a government economy drive.

The issue re-emerged as an item in the programme for the International Year of the Disabled in 1981, when a study group on residential care was convened with the objective of drawing up a manual of care practice which would assure a reasonable quality of life for those in residential units. It is unlikely, however, that any manual of practice which attracts general agreement could be in sufficiently specific terms as really to influence the conditions of disabled people in residential care. This is because needs of disabled people are as varied as the needs of any other group. It is as impossible to frame a precise yet widely applicable statement of what constitutes good residential care practice as it is to devise a precise and widely applicable code of good family life. What we can do is to identify certain principles of care, such as respect for privacy and the greatest possible measure of independence, the participation of those in residential units in deciding the policy and the priorities of the unit, and the role of the staff as enablers rather than custodians. The way these general principles are interpreted in practice in specific care situations will vary considerably according to the physical resources of the unit in question and the characteristics of the residents, especially whether their handicap is mental or physical. The best assurance that such interpretations will be made in a way to confer greatest benefit on the disabled residents lies in the training given to the residential care staff. The more professional they are, the more likely it is that they will use the knowledge, understanding and skill acquired in training to interpret the general principles of a caring environment in order to match the residential setting to the needs and wishes of the disabled resident.

There are, however, no prospects at present of the major commitment of resources which would be necessary if sufficient numbers of care staff are to be given a high enough level of appropriate training to enable them to make a real contribution to improvements in the quality of life in residential care. Although the desirability of more and better training for residential care staff is widely recognized, the priority accorded to this is low. The usual economic considerations applied to any proposal involving public expenditure, in accordance with the principle of economic rationality, indicate that money spent on raising staffing standards in residential units for the elderly or for incurably handicapped people could not be offset against any compensatory saving such as, for example, a speedier restoration of independent functioning. The gains expected to result are in the form of a better life for the residents, but these are non-material and non-calculable gains which cannot be objectively quantified in a form which easily justifies the commitment of public resources to such improvements at the expense of the many other desirable projects competing for public support. Residential care for the most dependent and vulnerable of our fellow citizens, who cannot hope for any improvement in their capacities for independence and self sufficiency, remains a Cinderella service for which no fairy godmother has yet appeared.

It is therefore not surprising to find that less than 10 per cent of all handicapped people are in institutional care of any kind. Among disabled people under retirement age only about 5 per cent are in institutional care, but among the elderly disabled population there are more people who have no relatives available to care for them at home, and the percentage in institutional care rises to nearer 13 per cent. It is clear, however, that the majority of both mentally handicapped and physically handicapped individuals of all ages are cared for in their own homes.

NOTES AND REFERENCES

1. P. TOWNSEND, *The Last Refuge*, Routledge & Kegan Paul (1962).
2. *Local Health and Social Service Statistics*, 1972–73 and 1973–74, published by The Chartered Institute of Public Finance and Accountancy and The Society of County Treasurers.
3. *Report of Royal Commission on the Law Relating to Mental Illness and Mental Deficiency*, Cmnd 169, HMSO, London (1957).
4. DHSS *Better Services for the Mentally Ill*, Cmnd 6233, HMSO, London (1975).
5. DHSS *Services for the Mentally Handicapped*, Cmnd 4683, HMSO, London (1971).
6. DHSS *Priorities for Health and Personal Social Services*, HMSO, London (1976).
7. J. TIZZARD AND J. C. GRAD, *The Mentally Handicapped and their Families*, Oxford University Press (1961).
8. *Report of the Committee of Enquiry into Mental Handicap Nursing and Care*, Cmnd 7468, HMSO, London (1979).
9. DHSS *Working Party on Manpower and Training for the Social Services*, DHSS, London (1976).
10. PERSONAL SOCIAL SERVICES COUNCIL, *Residential Care Reviewed*, London (1977).

Chapter eight
AT HOME WITH HANDICAP

The amount of help available to disabled people living at home with their families can crucially affect the quality of their lives. Before any sort of life at home is possible at all, there must be a dwelling which is physically capable of accommodating the handicapped member and his family. Most disabled people live in ordinary houses and flats with no special facilities, as was discovered in the survey conducted by the Office of Population Censuses and Surveys,[1] but it was also found that over a quarter of them endured very poor conditions, such as no accessible inside lavatory or having to sleep in the living room because the bedrooms could not be reached. The survey concluded that about a million disabled people living at home were in need of rehousing or substantial improvements to their existing dwellings.

For many years before the survey was conducted local housing authorities had been empowered to make special provision for disabled tenants. Few had chosen to do this in a way which involved the construction of specially designed units, and such special provision as was made usually amounted to reserving ground floor flats, or flats served by a lift, for disabled or elderly people with mobility problems. In 1970 the Chronically Sick and Disabled Persons Act put renewed emphasis on the responsibility of local housing authorities to make special provision for disabled people. Section 3 of the Act required local authorities to distinguish dwellings which were intended for disabled occupants from other dwellings when making their returns to central government specifying numbers of new housing units.

Further incentives were given to local housing authorities in the form of a special subsidy from the central government for each purpose-built dwelling specially constructed for a disabled occupant. Despite these measures, local authorities were slow to respond, and only about 4,000 specially designed housing units were built over the next ten years.[2] This was not due solely to parsimony, although the cost of such units was high and the government subsidy did not cover the additional expense occasioned by their special design. Other important considerations were those set out in a government circular which was despatched to housing authorities in 1974.[3] This reminded local authorities of their obligations regarding housing for disabled people but placed the greatest emphasis on disabled people's need for ordinary housing of a good standard of amenity. The circular stressed the fact, revealed by the survey of impaired people, that 85 per cent of disabled people were over fifty, and most lived in households of one or two persons. This meant that the larger family-type accommodation was rarely required by disabled people. The circular also pointed out that only 2 per cent of the adult disabled population was confined to a wheelchair although many more had some mobility problems. Therefore the circular urged local authorities to concentrate on upgrading the amenities in disabled people's existing homes, and on making available to disabled applicants suitable one- or two-bedroomed dwellings of standard design but with level access and, where necessary, ramped entrances. Ordinary council housing which was suitable for disabled occupants with only minor modifications, such as ramps, was given a new name – mobility housing,[4] and a small subsidy for each such unit completed was made available to local authorities from central government. The construction of specially designed units was relegated to a minor place in the programme for improving the housing of disabled people which was urged on local authorities in the 1974 circular.

Apart from the greater emphasis placed on helping disabled people to make adaptations to their existing homes, the policy urged by the 1974 circular really represented an endorsement of the earlier practice of earmarking ground floor flats and those served by lifts for disabled occupants. By 1974, however, local authorities were building far fewer high-rise blocks of flats with lifts, and were concentrating instead on two- or three-storey blocks where the upper floors were reached by stairs. The other main type of council housing provision was the two-storey house. Consequently only a small proportion of standard local authority building in 1974 was immediately obvious as suitable for disabled occupants with mobility problems. The criteria for dwellings to be accepted as of mobility standard were therefore modified to include two-storey houses where the staircase was straight and suitable for the fitting of a stair lift should the house be occupied by a disabled person unable to manage stairs. This amendment to the standard required of mobility housing meant that a great deal of ordinary modern council building could be made into mobility housing units with only simple modifications, such as ramped entrances and, very occasionally, a stair lift.

The ease with which local authorities could meet the requirements for the mobility housing subsidy certainly encouraged a rapid expansion of this type of provision, despite the fact that the subsidy was only £50 per unit to begin with and was not increased at a rate to keep pace with inflation. In addition, housing associations were encouraged to apply to the Treasury-financed Housing Corporation for grants to build mobility housing or convert existing housing to mobility standards for disabled tenants. By 1979, some 18,500 mobility-type dwellings had been completed or were under construction.[5] From that point onwards, however, local authorities were encouraged to sell council houses to the sitting tenants by the government which was returned in the general election in the spring of 1979. Encouragement became compulsion in the Housing Act 1980, except that the government responded to pressure from bodies concerned with the housing needs of particularly vulnerable groups in society, and exempted from the measure council properties specially built for elderly or disabled occupants.

However, the majority of council dwellings which, with minor modifications, could be made convenient for a disabled occupant, began their existence as standard units, part of the ordinary housing stock, occupied originally by people from the ordinary housing lists. These dwellings have no exemption from the requirements of the Housing Act 1980 and must be sold to the sitting tenant if he wants, and is able, to purchase. Local authorities were thus forced to deplete their stocks of housing units, including those with the potential to be made suitable, with minor modifications, for occupation by disabled people. At the same time the building of dwellings earmarked specially for elderly and disabled tenants was cut back in the interests of economy in public spending, making it inevitable that the gains in housing for handicapped people made during the years 1974–79 would soon be eroded.

Among the general population of Great Britain, the most common form of tenure, accounting for over half of all dwellings, is now owner occupation. About a third of the population lived in council housing at the time of the Housing Act 1980, and one fifth were housed in privately rented accommodation.

As mentioned above, 85 per cent of the disabled population is over fifty years of age, and the majority of these people established their marriages, homes and families before becoming disabled with increasing age. They are likely to manifest a similar pattern of tenure to that of the general population over fifty. In the survey of impaired people conducted by the Office of Population Censuses and Surveys in 1969, it was found that only about a third were owner occupiers, which reflected the fact that disabled people are concentrated in the older age groups, where home ownership has been less common. [6]In the decade since the survey, home ownership has become more widespread and is likely to be a more common feature than in the past among those becoming disabled in later life. We can assume, therefore, that somewhat more than one third of the disabled population of today are owner occupiers, although probably still not as high as the proportion (over 50%) which is found in Britain generally.

We cannot, however, also assume that all disabled people who are owner occupiers are uninterested in council housing policies. The survey in 1969 found that the dwellings owned by many of the elderly disabled respondents were of poor standard and lacking in basic amenities. A number of these owner occupiers were reported as being willing to exchange their form of tenure for that of a council tenant in a more convenient property. The same willingness may exist today among disabled owner occupiers with poor standard properties, particularly those who are elderly or living alone. Their prospects of council housing must be less since the Housing Act 1980.

HOUSING ADAPTATIONS

The disabled individual in owner occupation who has a husband or wife, and possibly still some family living at home, is more likely to be younger and to have better amenities. The advantages of owner occupation as a form of tenure will then be very apparent, particularly as a source of security to the able-bodied partner. For this group the most welcome assistance would probably be help in making additions or modifications to the existing home in order to add to the convenience or safety of the disabled occupant.

Local authorities had been empowered to give this sort of help to disabled people unable to pay the cost of such modifications themselves, under section 29 of the National Assistance Act 1946, but the use made of these permissive powers varied very considerably throughout the country.[7] In 1970, the obligation to provide aids and adaptations to disabled people in need of them was made mandatory in section 2 of the Chronically Sick and Disabled Persons Act. The Act laid the responsibility for this on the social services departments which were being reorganized in response to the recommendations of the Seebohm Report of 1969[8] and only became fully operative in 1971. Further local government reorganization in 1974 probably also hampered implementation of section 2. Housing departments, however, still retained their powers to make adaptations to the dwellings of disabled people. Perhaps because of this confusion of responsibility, local authorities failed to embark on any significant programme of housing modifications to assist disabled people. Although the number of minor adaptations made increased quite considerably after the Chronically Sick and Disabled Persons Act, and no doubt were greatly appreciated by the individual beneficiaries, less than 10 per cent of the adaptations involved the expenditure of more than £150. Even in the early 1970s, little in the way of major modifications or alterations could be made for under £150. Help with home adaptation in general amounted to no more than means-tested financial assistance with the provision of ramps, hand-rails and the installation of a gas or electric outlet to permit some form of heating other than an open fire. Major works, such as the installation of a stair-lift or constructing a downstairs lavatory, or widening doorways and improving circulation space, were rarely undertaken.

In 1978, Department of Environment Circular 59/78 was sent to local authorities reminding them of their responsibilities to give help with adaptations in the homes of disabled people. The Circular emphasized that the obligations imposed on social services departments by the Chronically Sick and Disabled Persons Act had not exempted the housing authorities from discharging their duties. An attempt was made in the Circular to resolve the confusion of obligations by charging housing departments with responsibility for structural modifications, giving as examples of these the installation of ramps, hand-rails, entryphone systems, remote control window openers, and equipping kitchens to wheelchair height. Local housing authorities undertaking such modifications in order to make a property suitable for a disabled occupant were eligible for a subsidy from central government. The social service departments were charged with the responsibility for providing non-structural aids to disabled people in need of them, and for assessing the home environment and circumstances in order to determine need for structural modifications.

Circular 59/78 proposed what seemed a sensible division of responsibilities but observance of its recommendations implied a considerable degree of co-operation and financial interdependence between housing departments and social services departments without any facilitating change in the statutory instruments under which both sets of departments continued to operate. In any case, the economic climate of the country worsened considerably shortly after the appearance of Circular 59/78, so that any improvements it might have effected in local authority efforts to adapt the housing of disabled people were lost in the budgetary cuts which followed.

Another function of housing authorities is to administer a system of grants payable to owners making improvements and alterations to their properties. Financial assistance in the form of an intermediate grant may be claimed from a housing department by the owner of a property who undertakes alterations to provide certain specified amenities, such as an indoor lavatory or a bathroom. In the case of a dwelling where there is a disabled occupant, an intermediate grant may be claimed even if an amenity exists already but is inaccessible to the disabled person. Such grants are available as of right, and normally cover half the agreed expense.

A grant known as an improvement grant may be payable, at the local housing authority's discretion, to cover half the cost of any approved alteration or enlargement undertaken by an owner to make a dwelling suitable for a disabled person. Under the Housing Act 1980, local authorities have discretion, in the case of applications in respect of improvements to benefit disabled people, to waive the normal limits on rateable values of property which will be eligible for improvement grants (fixed in 1980 at £225: £400 in the Greater London area).

A house owner who instals amenities or makes improvements, whether or not he is assisted by one of the above grants, usually increases the rateable value of his property and finds himself with a higher rate demand. Where the improvements have been necessary in order to meet the needs of a disabled person, there is provision for rate relief under the Rating (Disabled Persons) Act 1978. Applications for relief are made through the local valuation officer, who will decide whether to allow the claim on the grounds that the improvements were essential to permit the occupation of the property by the disabled person concerned. If the claim is allowed (and there is a right to appeal to the county court against refusal) there is a fixed scale of deductions from the standard rate demand. For example, where an additional bathroom has been provided, the deduction in 1980 was calculated on £20 according to the local rate in the pound.

Intermediate and improvement grants have probably been of greater financial help to owner occupiers of property where there is a disabled person than other schemes of assistance with adaptations. This is particularly likely in cases where the applicant's income puts him beyond means-tested assistance but has no effect on his eligibility for an intermediate or an improvement grant. It is possible for someone to apply both for one of these grants and also at the same time for help from his social services department under section 2 of the Chronically Sick and Disabled Persons Act. For example, an individual unable to bear his share of the cost of alterations could be assisted by the social services department.

DOMICILIARY SUPPORT AND CARE

The home help service was developed after the Second World War as a way of helping families through crises, such as at the birth of a baby or the temporary illness of the mother, and assisting those unable to manage their domestic chores to remain in their own homes. Over the years, the home help service has played a smaller and smaller part in giving help at the time of childbirth and by 1970 over 90 per cent of home help visits were made to elderly people, many of whom would be handicapped. Less than 6 per cent of their calls were to households with a disabled occupant under retirement age.

The home help service has clearly developed as a system of support for elderly people who, with a little domestic assistance, can continue to remain in their own homes, thus postponing or even avoiding altogether institutional admission. It is not, to any appreciable extent, a supporting service for disabled people and their families, because the sort of domestic assistance which the home help service is organized to provide is not the main need of most families coping with a disabled member. The help they need is assistance with, and regular respite from, the burden of giving personal care or supervision to their handicapped relative. The home help service was never introduced, and is simply not organized, to give this sort of personal attention, which is often required outside normal working hours.

The development of care services to support and relieve families looking after a disabled relative is not specifically provided for in any legislation, although local authorities could have interpreted the requirement contained in the Chronically Sick and Disabled Persons Act, to provide practical assistance to disabled people in their own homes, as a requirement to provide this sort of personal care service. It was left to voluntary initiative to make the first development in this sphere. The pioneer scheme, known as Crossroads, was started in Rugby about ten years ago with the help of a financial grant from an independent television company producing a long running serial of the same name in which a handicapped character appeared. The Crossroads scheme aimed to provide competent but non-professional care staff to help care for disabled people in their own homes in order to give relatives a rest, or to tide over a period when the person who normally gave care was ill or away on holiday. The service was an immediate success with disabled people and their families and further grants have been made, a number from statutory sources, to enable the Crossroads service to be continued and extended to several other areas of the country.

In addition, some similar schemes have been developed with money from the joint finances made available after 1976 to health authorities and social service departments for collaborative projects. At a time of severe limitation on the numbers who could be supported in institutional care, domiciliary care attendant schemes were seen by some authorities as an economical alternative to residential accommodation for even very severely handicapped people.

Although care attendant schemes have considerable potential to improve the quality of life for disabled people living at home, and their relatives, in practice they have an impact on very few at present. Availability of such help is very uneven throughout the country, and there can be no sanguine hopes that they will quickly become uniformly available. Experience has shown that services which are provided, like these, under permissive powers are particularly likely to show considerable variation from region to region, even at times when financial constraints are less severe than at present.

Apart from the home help service, and the small number of care attendant schemes, disabled people living at home who need some nursing care can be helped by the district nursing service provided by the health authorities. As in the case of the home help service, the vast majority of visits made by district nurses are to elderly people. The nursing care and health surveillance they give to these elderly patients, many of whom will be disabled, is enormously valuable. The district nursing service, however, plays only a small role in the care of younger disabled people living with their families. This is in no sense a criticism of the community nursing services, but merely reflects the fact that the type of personal care needed by younger handicapped people is not, in general, nursing care, and is not appropriately given as part of the district nursing services.

THE CHRONICALLY SICK AND DISABLED PERSONS ACT [DOC 3]

This Act has already been referred to at a number of points in this book, since it was a wide ranging measure with implications for many aspects of provision for disabled people. Section 2 of the Act was concerned to specify the type of services for handicapped citizens which local authorities were charged with a mandatory duty to provide to those in need of them. These were listed in section 2 as:

(i) practical assistance in the home, as, for example, the home help service
(ii) help to obtain wireless, television, library or similar recreational facilities
(iii) opportunities to attend lectures or educational courses, and to enjoy recreational outings and activities
(iv) help with travel arrangements for the purpose of (iii) above
(v) aids and adaptations in the home
(vi) holidays
(vii) meals, either at home or in clubs or centres
(viii) help with installing and equipping a telephone with the necessary attachments for use by a disabled person.

It is difficult to obtain a clear picture of the extent to which local authorities have provided the sort of services which were listed in section 2 of the Chronically Sick and Disabled Persons Act. This is because statistical information is not routinely available in respect of all items. The Department of Health and Social Security regularly publishes statistics of local authority personal social services[9] but these are not in a form which permits the identification of performances and expenditure in respect of each of the itemized services for disabled people. For example, figures are given of the numbers of people, expressed as a rate per thousand of the total population in the local authority area, receiving help with adaptations; with personal aids, television or radio (all lumped together); and with a telephone or attachments. There are no figures for the numbers of disabled people helped to obtain library or other recreational or educational facilities, and those assisted with meals or helped to go on holiday are not distinguished in the statistics from other groups of beneficiaries.

Although complete information is not, therefore, available, sufficient exists to make it clear that more disabled people have been helped by local authority services since the implementation of the Chronically Sick and Disabled Persons Act than was the case before. At the same time it is also evident that no local authority is meeting every request for services to disabled people, and it is also abundantly clear that there is still considerable variation between authorities in the amount of assistance offered to disabled citizens in respect of services which all authorities have had a mandatory duty to provide since 1970.

Local authority obligations under the Act

The Chronically Sick and Disabled Persons Act was clear and quite specific about the services and facilities which local authorities have a duty to provide for disabled people in need of them. It was not at all precise about the circumstances which would constitute need nor, even when need could be established, about the procedure to be followed if a local authority refused to discharge its obligations. Consequently, the extent to which local authorities have made services available to disabled people has continued to reflect fluctuating economic pressures and local variations in the commitment of resources to collective social provision.

Alf Morris, who drafted the Chronically Sick and Disabled Persons Act and became, in 1974, the country's first Minister for the Disabled, warned local authorities that once they acknowledged a disabled individual to have a need for a service listed in section 2 of the Act, it would be incumbent upon them to meet that need. He added that the discharge of their duties needed to be balanced with financial restraint.[10]

The loophole in the Chronically Sick and Disabled Persons Act was therefore clear to all local authorities. As long as they admitted only such need as they had resources to meet, they could comply with the letter of the Act and still keep within budgetary limits. Consequently, as the 1970s progressed and social services budgets became tighter, local authorities became correspondingly more cautious about admitting a disabled person's need for a service. No procedure for appealing against a local authority's refusal to acknowledge a need was established in the Chronically Sick and Disabled Persons Act, so the mandatory nature of services listed in the Act has proved utterly ineffectual in avoiding limitations or even reductions in provision which an authority deems it expedient to make in the light of financial consideration.

Access

Another area where the Chronically Sick and Disabled Persons Act sought to effect improvement in the lives of disabled people was that of increasing the physical accessibility of community facilities. Local authorities were required to issue those of its disabled citizens with mobility problems with a special badge which could be displayed in the car driven or regularly used by the disabled person. Most authorities have made special parking provisions and concessions for badge holders. These vary from area to area but seem to be uniformly appreciated, although some developments of vehicle-free shopping precincts have failed to make special provision for those with the disabled car user's badge and, however welcome precincts may be in other respects, have eroded the value of the badge.

The failure of some of those planning shopping precincts to take account of the way disabled people would be affected is all the more remarkable because other clauses of the Chronically Sick and Disabled Persons Act required property developers erecting new buildings or making substantial modifications to existing ones, to which the public would have access, to give consideration to the needs of disabled people. Once again, however, as in the case of the services which local authorities were required to provide, the Act contained no procedures for enforcement. It might still be that, even without powers of enforcement, the mere existence of the Act would encourage property developers in most cases to ensure that facilities were accessible to disabled people. Clearly the Minister for the Disabled, Alf Morris, had his doubts on this score, and in 1977 he appointed a committee to enquire into access facilities for disabled people. It was known as the Silver Jubilee Committee, to commemorate the twenty-fifth anniversary of the accession of Queen Elizabeth II to the throne, and after two years of investigation the committee submitted its report in 1979.[11]

The Silver Jubilee Committee had found that there was widespread ignorance of the Act among property developers, and concluded that the Chronically Sick and Disabled Persons Act had had little effect in improving access for disabled people. The Report suggested that the failure to make provision for the needs of disabled people was more often due to thoughtless disregard than to a conscious decision to exclude them, and urged that more publicity be given to the requirements of the Act. At the same time the Report noted that there was at present no way of compelling a developer to make reasonable provision for the needs of disabled people if he chose not to do so, since planning permission could not be withheld on these grounds. In order to make control effective, the Department of the Environment would need to include in the building regulations with which development must comply a requirement that the British Standard Code of Practice (revised in 1979) on access for disabled people must be observed. At present buildings to which the public are admitted must comply with fire and safety regulations but not, so far, with the Code of Practice on access. The Silver Jubilee Committee noted that compliance with fire and safety regulations had had the effect of making buildings less accessible to disabled people, and urged that building regulations themselves should be framed having regard to the needs of disabled people.

The Silver Jubilee Committee was disbanded after making its report, but it was quite clear that access problems for disabled people remained acute and had even been exacerbated by some actions and legislation, such as the fire and safety regulations, which were not directly discriminatory against disabled people but had a discriminatory effect. Consequently a successor to the Silver Jubilee Committee was appointed by Alf Morris as one of his last actions before ceasing to be Minister for the Disabled after the general election of 1979. The new committee was known as the Committee on Restrictions against Disabled People (CORAD) and its brief was to examine the whole issue of discrimination, whether intentional or not, against the full participation of disabled people in community life.

As nothing effective has yet been done in respect of the specific difficulties highlighted in the Silver Jubilee Report, there seems no reason to expect that any prompt and determined action will be taken to combat any discrimination, however widespread, against disabled people which may be exposed by CORAD.

COMMUNITY CARE

The majority of handicapped people have probably always lived in private households in the community, but this is likely to be particularly true nowadays. The pendulum of provision for most of the vulnerable groups in society, including handicapped people, has swung away from institutional care since the Second World War and towards community care. This is manifest in the rejection of the large children's homes for children in care and the concentration instead on fostering or family regeneration and support. It is evident, too, in the reduced proportion of elderly people in residential care compared with earlier years in the century. It was also a factor in shaping the mental health legislation of 1959, and has played a part in the development of services for handicapped people.

This chapter, and many points in preceding chapters, however, serve to show that community services for the handicapped have not developed at a rate to provide an alternative system of care to institutional provision. The level of supporting services currently available to most handicapped people and their families means that there is not so much community care as community neglect. Fortunately, families are generally more financially secure since the Second World War, due to social security provisions, and they have proved able and willing to shoulder an increased burden of care for dependent members.

Where a disabled person is without a family able to give care and support, then living at home with a handicap can mean a deprived and isolated existence despite legislation which many believed would ensure vastly improved life styles for our disabled people. The reasons for the failure to eradicate the social disadvantages of disability are discussed in part three.

NOTES AND REFERENCES

1. J. BUCKLE, *Work and Housing of Impaired People in Great Britain*, HMSO, London (1971).
2. *Housing and Construction Statistics No. 29*, First Quarter 1979, HMSO, London.
3. DEPARTMENT OF ENVIRONMENT, *Circular 74/74*.

4. SELWYN GOLDSMITH, *Mobility Housing*, Conference Proceedings of the 2nd European Conference of Rehabilitation International, NAIDEX Kent (1978).
5. *Housing and Construction Statistics No. 29*, *op. cit.*
6. J. BUCKLE, *op. cit.*
7. For a fuller discussion of regional variations, see E. TOPLISS AND B. GOULD, *Charter for the Disabled*, Basil Blackwell & Martin Robertson, Oxford (1981).
8. *Report of the Committee on Local Authority and Allied Personal Social Services* Cmnd 3703, HMSO, London (1968).
9. DHSS, *Personal Social Services Statistics.*
10. *H. C. Deb*, Vol. 904, Cols. *235–6.*
11. *Silver Jubilee Committee Report on Improving Access for Disabled People, Can Disabled People Go Where You Go*?, DHSS, London (1979).

Part three
RATIONALITY IN SOCIAL POLICY

Chapter nine

1970 – THE WATERSHED

In the review of policies for disabled people given in the preceding chapters, mention has frequently been made of the Chronically Sick and Disabled Persons Act 1970, the sections of which ranged over many aspects of life for handicapped people and their families [doc 3].

The breadth of purpose of this Act, never before paralleled in measures concerning disabled people, makes the year 1970 something of a watershed in the development of social policy for the handicapped. Not only did the Chronically Sick and Disabled Persons Act break new ground by attempting, in one comprehensive measure, to improve the welfare of disabled people in so many ways, including schooling, housing, institutional care, supporting services in the community, access to public places and representation on policy-making bodies, but it was followed in the decade ahead by a veritable explosion of legislation,[1] reports and enquiries[2] affecting disabled people.

It would, however, be a mistake to regard 1970 as marking any fundamental change in social attitudes towards disability, or radical change of direction in social policy. On the contrary, a careful examination of the way in which the Chronically Sick and Disabled Persons Act has been implemented,[3] and of the implications and effects of subsequent legislation and provision, suggests that while the position of disabled people in the 1980s is better than it was before the improvements made in the 1970s, their disadvantages relative to the able-bodied majority, which also enhanced its living standards during the same period, remain broadly unchanged.

STIGMA

In particular, disabled people still complain about being stigmatized by public attitudes which label them as inferior, imputing a generalized inadequacy because of a particular, albeit sometimes severe, functional loss. It is argued that it is often man-made barriers, both physical and psychological, which deny disabled people the chance to use their residual capacities to the full. This was made very clear in a report published by the Department of Health and Social Security in 1979[4] which emphasized the considerable restrictions imposed on disabled people due to public disregard to their special needs.

The Committee on Restrictions Against Disabled People (CORAD) was subsequently formed to investigate ways of reducing such discrimination. Its chairman, Mr Peter Large, himself disabled when a young man, focused the work of his committee on the need to change public attitudes, which he saw as posing the gravest threat to the full development and integration into society of disabled people. He certainly did not mean, and no one could seriously suggest, that the public in general lacks compassion for those who are disabled. It is not inhumanity or callous contempt which leads to the exclusion of disabled people from so many spheres of activity, but rather that the social and occupational patterns which predominate in our society are geared to rational strategies for economic development, and these favour the energetic, intelligent, independent and ambitious individual with vigorous good health.

Respect for such qualities is accordingly fostered both consciously and unconsciously through our socialization and educational processes. We train our children to become independent and competitive, and to value their health and an attractive, wholesome appearance, because in this way we will best prepare them to fit successfully into adult society and the world of work, which is of such central importance. The more effectively people in general are socialized to respect individual achievement, so heavily emphasized by the modern rejection of nepotism in favour of more equal opportunities for individual competition for success in life, the more likely it is that physical or mental disabilities which limit personal independence and restrict achievements will be seen as a badge of imperfection and inadequacy affecting all spheres of life.

This, of course, is the unfavourable public image, or stigmatization, of disability of which disabled people complain. It encourages the perception of a handicapped individual primarily in terms of his disability and what he cannot do, thus serving to justify society's failure to facilitate his fullest possible participation in the community and the maximum development of his remaining capacities.

This negative view of disabled people affects their personal and social relationships as well as their opportunities to participate in the economic life of the community, since the stigma of disability devalues the disabled individual for the roles of friend or marriage partner. The general perception of an 'eligible' bachelor, or an 'attractive' girl rests heavily on assessing the appearance, individual competence and occupational prospects of the particular person, so that a disabled man or woman is not perceived as eligible or attractive. The extent to which this sort of social stigma creates problems of isolation and emotional and sexual frustration for disabled young people has been increasingly acknowledged in recent years, but effective social policies to help are still lacking. It is, in any case, doubtful whether as a society we really wish to change the public attitudes which underlie the stigmatization of disability, since these same attitudes also help to uphold much of what we value. We do not, however, even provide adequate counselling services for disabled people and their families to help them adjust to their painful situation, nor have we devoted sufficient resources to give appropriate training to those who staff residential units accommodating disabled people in order that they should be able to understand the emotional problems of disablement as well as the physical need for care which it creates.

In the sphere of economic and community activity, the negative view of disability which is the widespread consequence of our prevailing hierarchy of values often leads to action which, albeit unintentionally, further isolates disabled people. For example, the proliferation of self-service petrol stations did not occur because of any conscious decision to make life more difficult for the disabled motorist, although this has been the effect. It was simply that, in considering the likely reactions to unattended pumps by the consumer public, the fact that many disabled people could and did drive cars was overlooked and disregarded in assessing the economic good sense of arguments for the change to self-service. Another example of unintentionally discriminatory action was that relating to fire and safety regulations incorporated in building regulations. The heavy fire doors, and the prohibition of the use of lifts in the event of fire, rendered inaccessible a number of buildings which were previously convenient for the employment, habitation or recreational use of disabled people, thus further restricting their activities and opportunities. Once again, the discriminatory effect was the consequence not of a conscious decision to exclude disabled people but of the negative view of disability which encouraged the decision-makers to overlook the fact that among the potential workers, or theatre patrons, or shoppers, would be some people with disabilities, and so their needs were simply not considered when framing the fire and safety regulations for the benefit of the able-bodied majority.

It was in order to minimize such thoughtless discrimination that the Chronically Sick and Disabled Persons Act had made provision for a disabled person, or one knowledgeable about the needs and circumstances of disabled people, to be included on a number of national committees involved in planning and policy-making in spheres which directly affected the welfare of handicapped people. In addition, the Act required local authorities to appoint at least one disabled member to any committee concerned with issues affecting the welfare of handicapped persons and where the membership was not restricted to elected councillors.

However honourably these requirements may have been discharged (and complete information on this point is not available) it is clear from the examples of unintentional discrimination given above that, if disabled people are really to be full members of society, their interests are involved in practically every social act and decision, however apparently unrelated to the issue of disability. To make statutory provision for disabled people to have a spokesman on certain committees specifically concerned with matters which clearly affect their welfare is doubtless an important step towards ensuring a better match between the provisions which are made and the needs articulated by disabled people, but it does not challenge the fundamental assumption that social arrangements will primarily reflect the interests and capacities of the majority of the population – in other words, the non-disabled.

It is, indeed, logically impossible to reduce the primacy of the able-bodied majority, since impairments are only recognized as disabling handicaps if they seriously affect the ability of an individual relative to most others in the community. Social arrangements therefore are geared to the capacities common to most people throughout most of their adult lives. While the particular type or degree of impairment which disables a person for full participation in society may change, it is inevitable that there will always be a line, somewhat indefinite but none the less real, between the able-bodied majority and a disabled minority whose interests are given less salience in the activities of society as a whole.

Similarly the values which underpin society must be those which support the interests and activities of the majority, hence the emphasis on vigorous independence and competitive achievement, particularly in the occupational sphere, with the unfortunate spin-off that it encourages a stigmatizing and negative view of disabilities which handicap individuals in these valued aspects of life. Because of the centrality of such values in the formation of citizens of the type needed to sustain the social arrangements desired by the able-bodied majority, they will continue to be fostered by family upbringing, education and public esteem. By contrast, disablement which handicaps an individual in these areas will continue to be negatively valued, thus tending towards the imputation of general inferiority to the disabled individual, or stigmatization.

The effect of stigma on disabled people has been examined by Erving Goffman.[5] He observed that there was widespread avoidance of disabled people by the non-disabled, manifest in such strategies as appearing not to notice a disabled person, or selecting a seat as far as possible away from a disabled person in the same room. In discussions involving both disabled and non-disabled participants which Goffman studied, he noted that the able-bodied people would rarely criticize or disagree strongly with any statements made by a disabled person, thus implying that physical impairment affected capacity for vigorous argument and ability to withstand criticism. Goffman was mainly concerned with the way stigmatized individuals managed their situation, or their 'spoiled identity' as he called it. This focus reflects Goffman's view of human interaction as a sort of contest where each party is trying to present his own personality in the most favourable light, at the expense, if necessary, of discrediting his partner in the transaction. One does not need to accept Goffman's rather jaundiced view of the development and presentation of self in order to find interesting and illuminating his examples of the way disabled individuals become aware of being stigmatized and react to that realization.

Goffman is not particularly concerned with why some personal attributes should be stigmatized and not others, but in concluding his analysis of responses to stigma he comments that the perception of particular personal properties as desirable or undesirable seems to have a social function.[6] We have sought, in this chapter, to identify the social function served by the hierarchy of prestige attaching to personal qualities in western society. We have suggested that personal health and active vigour are valued for the part they play in facilitating the successful achievement of social status in competition with others. Conversely, impairments which handicap individuals in such achievements are defined as disabilities and are regarded as undesirable and, in Goffman's language, 'deeply discrediting' personal attributes.

It is unrealistic to expect that people defined as disabled because their impairments handicap them in the socially crucial spheres of personal independence and occupational performances should then be evaluated according to a different set of values which attaches the greatest esteem and importance to the attributes which their impairments do not affect, such as, for example, patience, cheerfulness or artistic sensitivity. Not only is it unrealistic, but any attempt to apply such different value standards only emphasizes the social marginality of disabled people and segregates them more completely from the mainstream of society.

The stigma of disability, in the sense that society tends to impute a generalized inferiority to those with disabling impairments, is an inevitable corollary of the fact that disablement is a relative and socially defined condition based primarily on assessment of competence for the world of work.

SOCIAL STATUS AND WORK

The paramountcy of the occupational sphere in modern society is demonstrated by the value attached to work for its own sake, and not merely as a means to survival. Work is seen by most people as intrinsically worthwhile, even as a moral duty. This is taken so much for granted in modern industrial societies that we are apt to regard the work ethic as basic human nature. Yet such an attitude is by no means universal but appears to be the result of careful indoctrination and socialization processes undertaken in western industrial societies in order to foster a commitment to regular and unremitting work far in excess of that needed for subsistence, because without such a commitment, modern industrial societies could not survive.

One strand in the formation of this commitment has been the cultivation of higher and yet higher material expectations, so that the worker always has a goal just out of reach, towards which he will continue to work and strive even after he has earned enough to provide for the necessities of life for himself and his family.[7]

The other strand has been the cultivation of the notion of work as a moral duty, or a 'calling' of comparable moral worth to a religious calling.[8] The following hymn, regularly sung by little children in a primary school morning assembly service in recent years, is just one example of the way in which the view of work as a moral duty is inculcated:

Jesus let me do work in school for you,
Numbers, handwork, reading –
All the things I shall be needing
If I am to do useful work for you
With obedient mind
I will seek to find
All the things I should be knowing
All the time that I am growing
If I am to do happy work for you.

A CULTURE OF LEISURE AS AN ALTERNATIVE TO WORK

The significance of productive activity is so overriding in our society today that not to obtain gainful employment tends to be seen by the individuals concerned as well as by others, as in large part a moral failure and therefore a reflection on their worth as citizens. Even being a housewife and mother is not valued as an activity which contributes to the wealth of the nation, and married women who do not also work outside the home are increasingly likely to be described, and to describe themselves, as 'of no occupation' or 'only a housewife'.

Similarly, whereas in previous centuries considerable respect was accorded to those possessing sufficient wealth to make it unnecessary for them to work, little prestige nowadays attaches to the 'idle rich', the 'wealthy playboy' or the 'gentleman of leisure'. These are all equivocal or critical labels, and the wealthy person today has to earn respect by being employed in a capacity which society is prepared to recognize as worthwhile. To have only hobbies, however cultured or absorbing, merits little respect, and the person who expresses his skill and wisdom only in leisure activities is called somewhat contemptuously a dilettante, whereas similar abilities applied in the performance of paid employment would merit the title of 'expert' and an accordingly high social esteem.

The plain fact is that the emphasis on the importance of regular employment characteristic of advanced economies is incompatible with a culture which gives high prestige to leisure. Instead of associating leisure activities with wealth, status and desirable personal circumstances and qualities, we now associate non-work chiefly with ageing, indolence and incompetence, incapacity or the misfortune of unemployment – none of them circumstances which the community in general is anxious to emulate.

During the period of high unemployment at the beginning of the 1980s, arguments were advanced to the effect that a high level of unemployment was likely to be the norm for industrial societies in the future, and therefore more value should be accorded to leisure activities if those unable to find work were to retain their self-respect. Whatever the accuracy of the predictions of continuing high unemployment, no strong emphasis on the value of leisure activities has begun to emerge. Indeed, in Britain the reaction to the very high rates of unemployment among school-leavers – a group which has had the shortest exposure to the work ethic and was therefore most likely to be receptive to a new code of values which esteemed leisure activities – was to re-emphasize the importance of work. Official intervention to encourage employment opportunities was heavily concentrated on school-leavers, with the avowed intention of minimizing the risks of their developing an unemployment culture where they became content not to be employed.

Far from leading to a devaluation of occupational achievement, economic recession only emphasized the need for individual competitiveness in securing employment. A young disabled person, therefore, is likely to experience even more difficulty in finding work in the competitive conditions of high unemployment and an even greater sense of inadequacy if he fails. What he is unable to achieve in the sphere of gainful employment will continue to be more significant in the eyes of society than anything he may be able to do in other spheres, a bitter realization that causes much distress to disabled people.

SOCIAL POLICY AND PUBLIC ATTITUDES

Our argument so far has been that public attitudes which both emphasize and aggravate the handicaps of disabled people have not changed fundamentally, despite an increase in legislative provision, since 1970. The explanation of the public concern for the welfare of disabled people given expression in the burst of social policy after 1970 is not to be found in any remarkable change of values. Indeed, we have suggested that any such change, which would belittle the incapacities resulting from disablement and instead accord social esteem to the unimpaired functions, is logically impossible, because to place greater value on a person's unimpaired functions than on those which are impaired would in effect be to re-designate him as not disabled at all according to the values of his society. The truth of this proposition is well illustrated by H. G. Wells' story of an isolated society where blindness was hereditary and normal, so that when a sighted stranger literally crash-landed among them, he was regarded as handicapped by his abnormal physical condition.[9]

The pain of disablement which results from negative public attitudes towards the person unable to compete as vigorously or successfully as the majority, especially in the sphere of employment, remains undiminished after all the statutes, reports and enquiries. None the less, it is a fact that disabled people are more evident in our society today than they were twenty or thirty years ago, and more consideration is given to the interests of the handicapped population than used to be the case. If this is not to be explained by any modifications in the value patterns which emphasize what disabled people cannot do rather than what they might achieve, what can be the explanation?

A close scrutiny of the way in which social policy in respect of handicapped people has developed suggests that the needs of the disabled minority have in general been met by collective provision when their interests have been seen as compatible with or conducive to furthering the well-being of society as a whole. That well-being is seen primarily in terms of national economic performance, so that social policies to advance the welfare of disabled people are proposed, considered and decided upon in the light of an evaluation of the economic costs and benefits for society as a whole implied by the proposed measure. Provision which is seen to be economically rational in the sense of leading to an overall increment in the well-being of society, and not merely to an improvement in the conditions of a disabled minority at the expense of the interests of the majority, will command the necessary commitment of public resources for implementation. Policies which seek to subordinate the interests of the majority to improving the conditions and opportunities of the disabled minority are unlikely to be enacted or, if enacted, successfully implemented, as a study of the effects of existing legislation will indicate.

ECONOMIC RATIONALITY AND EDUCATIONAL POLICIES FOR HANDICAPPED CHILDREN

The earliest pieces of legislation to focus specifically on handicap were those at the end of the last century concerning the education of blind, deaf and mentally defective children. They followed the report of a Royal Commission which strongly emphasized the need to make special provision for the education of these children in order to minimize the risks of their growing up unable to find any employment and becoming a permanent burden on the state. In the more strident (or more honest) materialism of the nineteenth century, it was not even felt necessary to conceal the economic considerations which prompted the recommendation of special educational provision behind any expressions of concern for the disabled children and their hopes and aspirations. The report bluntly stated: 'The blind, deaf and dumb, and the educable class of imbeciles form a distinct group, which, if left uneducated, become not only a burden to themselves, but a weighty burden to the State. It is the interest of the State to educate them, so as to dry up as far as possible the minor streams which ultimately swell the great torrent of pauperism.'[10]

More recent educational provision for handicapped children has been framed with just as acute an awareness of economic considerations, even if these have been given less direct emphasis in statements made for public consumption. We noted in Chapter 2, for example, that a major consideration in framing the Education (Handicapped Children) Act 1970 was the need to make better use of existing facilities. It removed the distinction between 'training' for the 'ineducable' and 'education' for the 'educable but subnormal', translating at a stroke all the junior training centres existing in National Health Service premises for the 'ineducable' children into special schools, thus eliminating any shortage of special school places. It is true that the transfer of responsibility for the school thus acquired did in fact lead to some improvement in facilities and resources, because the Department of Education encouraged higher standards of space per child and more resources than had existed in the junior training centres under National Health Service administration. An important argument made for such improvements was that although children of severely subnormal intelligence were very slow learners, large numbers of them could, with appropriate techniques and skilled teachers, be taught basic social and personal skills which would equip them to live at home rather than be cared for permanently, and more expensively, in an institution.

The emphasis on economic considerations when framing educational policies for handicapped children was also apparent in the proposals made in 1980 for special educational provision, and which were referred to in Chapter 2. The school placement of a handicapped child, it was proposed, should be decided mainly on consideration of cost to the public purse and the educational interests of other children. The interests of the handicapped child were as certainly subordinated to economic considerations in 1980 as they had been in the recommendation of the Royal Commission in 1889.

ECONOMIC RATIONALITY AND EMPLOYMENT POLICIES FOR HANDICAPPED PEOPLE

In this sphere of social policy the emphasis has again been on committing effort and resources primarily in ways which will increase the employment potential of the maximum number of disabled people for the least cost. Obviously it makes better economic sense to concentrate on provisions which will assist those who, although handicapped in finding and keeping work, could, with some assistance, be expected to earn a living and become self-supporting rather than dependent on public money. Hence the employment rehabilitation services concentrate on the younger and less disabled persons who are most likely to find employment on the open market or, failing this, to be reasonably productive in sheltered working conditions. A scheme for providing home employment for those who were so severely disabled that they were not even acceptable for sheltered workshops was tried some years ago but quickly lost the support of the Department of Employment (as it then was called) because it cost more money to provide such severely disabled people with work than could be recovered from the sale of their output.

As the review of the employment policies made in Chapter 4 concluded, it is hardly surprising that rational economic criteria should govern the type of assistance given to a disabled person in employment, which is the economic sphere of society. What is less readily understood, however, is that the same tests of economic rationality are applied to all provisions for disabled people, even to those which ostensibly involve the commitment of public resources for no purpose other than to improve the quality of life for the recipient of the benefit.

ECONOMIC RATIONALITY AND FINANCIAL SUPPORT FOR HANDICAPPED PEOPLE

At first sight it would seem that financial benefits paid to disabled people out of taxation represent an instance of the expenditure of public funds in response to the acceptance of a moral duty, with no calculative considerations at all. Yet some explanation needs to be sought of the different levels of financial provision made for people with the same degree of disablement. In Chapter 6 we listed the different forms of financial support available, and it was stressed that while compensation for the functional loss sustained was a fundamental feature of both the Services pension scheme and the industrial injury scheme, it played no part in the National Insurance contributory or non-contributory invalidity pensions, nor in the supplementary benefit provisions. In the case of disability pensions for the services, these rights exist as part of the condition of engagement and are presumably deemed to be necessary if sufficient recruits of the requisite calibre are to be attracted to enlist, rather than to follow some other career. A service career must be seen to be comparable with civilian employment in the overall balance of advantages and disadvantages – thus the rather rigid disciplinary requirements of service life are balanced by the material security the job offers, and the greater risk of being involved in physically hazardous undertakings is balanced by the generosity of the pension provisions. These are rational economic considerations and so also, at bottom, is the argument that the disabled serviceman deserves more generous support from the community than does a similarly handicapped person whose disabilities were caused in some other way. This is once again saying that in order to motivate servicemen to give the right degree of commitment to their duties they must be assured that their contribution will be highly valued by society, and this is best demonstrated by the pay and conditions for service personnel which society is prepared to finance.

Similarly the industrial injury scheme suggests that the public recognizes civilian employment as an activity slightly less valuable to the well-being of the community than defending the nation's safety and sovereignty (at least in peacetime). Consequently disablement resulting from industrial injury merits greater public support than the same degree of incapacity attributable to non-industrial causes. This reinforces the central value of work which, it has been repeatedly argued, is of vital importance to the maintenance of our society as we know it.

When it comes to those whose disabilities are the result of factors other than service or civilian employment, financial support is given to avoid destitution. The arguments for the relief of destitution have for many years been couched in terms of economic rationality. Edwin Chadwick, the principle architect of the Poor Law Reform Act 1834 and an arch-exponent of utilitarian economic measures, noted that much disease emanated from the squalor of poverty and caused yet more ill health and pauperization. He commented that nearly half the children born to poor families living in the Manchester area in the 1830s died before they were old enough to work and be of any productive value to the community.[11]

Chadwick's analysis of the consequence of destitution for society as a whole, as well as for the unfortunate individuals concerned, received confirmation in the great poverty surveys conducted at the turn of the century. These particularly emphasized the disastrous effect on the nation's future workforce and military potential of allowing widespread poverty to go unalleviated. The notion that the stability and health of our society would be jeopardized if pockets of destitution were left to fester unrelieved in our midst has importantly affected public readiness to commit resources to the relief of destitution. The National Insurance contributory pension schemes arose out of the recognition of certain states as being likely to lead to destitution. Old age, widowhood, sickness and unemployment were identified as states sufficiently common to merit collective provision to avoid the destitution they otherwise threatened. Permanent disability was only recognized in 1971 as a major cause of lack of earnings and a National Insurance invalidity pension was introduced. This takes no account of degree of incapacity, but is simply an income maintenance payment for those whose working life is ended by disability of any kind or degree.

In the case of the attendance allowance, considerations of economic rationality were quite explicit. It was hoped that payment of an attendance allowance would enable more very severely disabled people to be looked after at home rather than seek admission to scarce and expensive residential or hospital care. The economic factors which underlie the pressures towards care in the community were touched upon in Chapter 6, which discusses residential care policies for handicapped people. Two main advantages are claimed for community care – one, that it is cheaper, and two, that most handicapped people and their families prefer it. The first claim depends upon keeping supporting services in the community to a minimum, and the second depends to a considerable extent on keeping residential care alternatives so unattractive and institutionalized that handicapped people continue to see life in a private household, whatever its burdens, privations and limitations, as preferable. The principle of less eligibility is still with us, and demand for residential accommodation from disabled people can be kept economically low providing the forms of accommodation offered are seen to be less eligible than almost any way of life in a private household.

ECONOMIC RATIONALITY AND COMMUNITY SUPPORT FOR HANDICAPPED PEOPLE

The main policy instruments for the provision of supporting services to handicapped people are the National Assistance Act 1948 [doc 12] and the Chronically Sick and Disabled Persons Act 1970 [doc 3]. Both are measures formed with the ostensible purpose of meeting individual need but, as Chapter 7 has shown, neither has been effective in ensuring that need as perceived by the disabled individual and his family will in fact be acknowledged or met. Although the 1970 Act imposed statutory obligations on local authorities, the circumstances in which they were called upon to discharge these obligations were not specified, and central government pronouncements since the Act was passed have emphasized that authorities are expected to balance the claims of disabled people against the cost to the community as a whole. This is entirely consistent with the arguments which were originally advanced in support of the measure, when it was stressed that it would make good economic sense to devote public resources to keeping disabled people in their own homes and as independent and productive as possible, as in this way the greater expense of total dependency and institutional care could be avoided. It is therefore not surprising if economic considerations should be found to make it impossible to comply with all the requests for assistance made by disabled people living at home.

ECONOMIC RATIONALITY AND THE SOCIAL RESPONSE TO HANDICAP

The emphasis on economically rational policies does not appear to be seen as a matter for regret or apology by politicians of any persuasion, nor even by disabled people themselves and associations concerned to promote their welfare. On the contrary, it is most often seen as a goal towards which social policies are rightly orientated – although there may be disagreement over what constitutes economically rational action in any given context. In 1980, government proposals for economies in health and welfare expenditure were criticized in an official report, not on grounds of inequity or lack of humanity but because of economic irrationality. It was pointed out that the cuts which it was proposed to make in some areas would only increase pressures on other areas which were more expensive to operate. The report commented sternly:

> 'We are struck by the apparent lack of strategic policy-making at the DHSS; the failure to examine the overall impact of changes in expenditure levels and changes in the social environment across the various services and programmes for which the Department is responsible.
>
> The Committee wishes to record its disappointment and dismay at the continuing failure of the DHSS to adopt a coherent policy strategy. . . .'[12]

Although, therefore, there is room for argument and debate as to what measures are most economically rational and effective, it is the main thesis of this book that considerations of economic rationality best explain why particular policies in respect of handicapped people have developed in the form, and at the time, they have, and the way in which they have been implemented or circumvented.

This, of course, relates to the theory of social policy development in general, and in the next chapter we look more closely at the concept of economic rationality in the context of explaining social policy.

NOTES AND REFERENCES

1. See the chronological list of legislation on p. 180.
2. See the chronological list of reports on p. 181–2 and of enquiries on p. 183.
3. For a detailed study of the Chronically Sick and Disabled Persons Act 1970, its genesis, its passage through Parliament and

its implementation, see E. TOPLISS AND B. GOULD, *Charter for the Disabled*, Basil Blackwell & Martin Robertson, Oxford (1981).

4. *Silver Jubilee Committee Report on Improving Access for Disabled People, Can Disabled People Go Where You Go?*, DHSS, London (1979).
5. E. GOFFMAN, *Stigma: Notes on the Management of a Spoiled Identity*, Prentice Hall, New Jersey (1963).
6. *Ibid.*
7. See, for example, V. PACKARD, *The Wastemakers*, Longman, London (1961).
8. See MAX WEBER, *The Protestant Ethic and the Spirit of Capitalism*, George Allen & Unwin, London (1930).
9. H. G. WELLS, *The Country of the Blind*, Odhams Press, London (n.d.).
10. *Report of the Royal Commission on the Blind, the Deaf and Dumb, etc. of the United Kingdom*, 1889, C 5781, Vol. xix.
11. *Report of the Royal Commission on the Health of Towns*, 1845.
12. The Government White Papers on Public Expenditure: *The Social Services, Third Report from the Social Services Committee*, Session 1979–80, Vol. 1, HMSO, London (1980).

Chapter ten
EXPLAINING SOCIAL POLICY

Until quite recently the development of social policy has been treated largely descriptively, giving more or less full and accurate accounts of the various measures included in the term 'social policy', and outlining the chronological sequence in which such measures occurred.

This is still an important aspect of knowledge for any student of social policy, but there is an increasing emphasis on *explaining* social policy – on analysing the reasons for it taking the form it does at the time it does. Some explanation is, of course, implied in any historical treatment of the subject. Nearly every English student of social policy, for instance, has heard that the Boer War of 1899–1902 revealed a very low standard of physical health among the young men who volunteered to fight, and that this awareness was a causal factor in the introduction of school meals for needy children in 1906[1] and school medical inspections in 1907.[2]

History is defined by the Oxford English Dictionary as 'a continuous methodical record' and, in order to make such a record, some analytical judgement is essential to determine which of the myriad of happenings in a large society do in fact constitute the antecedents of any given phenomenon. In a historical account of social policy, therefore, the emphasis is on discrete past events and the way in which they have shaped specific measures of social welfare.

This approach, while a valuable component of the study of social policy, tends to present the subject as a series of sequential developments in, for example, housing, or education, or health care, without any real consideration of the overall rationale of welfare policy, or of the interaction between social policy measures and the structure and processes of the wider society within which they occur.

These latter considerations are, of course, the sphere of sociology rather than history. Sociological explanations of social policy are quite small in volume and mostly recent.[3] The rising interest in sociological analysis of social policy doubtless has many causes, but a contributing factor must have been the growing body of historical and descriptive material relating to welfare measures in a variety of countries. This has facilitated comparative studies, which in turn have led to an awareness that although there are differences between countries with regard to their social policies, there are also similarities despite their very diverse histories and political systems. Accounts of social policy development in terms of historical antecedents were therefore recognized as lacking an important dimension of explanation.

At the same time as descriptive studies of social policy measures were accumulating, there were also increasing numbers of sociological studies of the effects of certain welfare measures. A considerable body of material had been gathered, for example, on the way in which the Education Act 1944, which made secondary education free for all children, had affected the educational opportunities of, particularly, the children of the lowest income groups.[4] Information was also being gathered on the extent to which health care services, free at the point of delivery under the National Health Service Act 1946, had eliminated differences in health, and health service utilization, between different social groups.[5] In relation to financial measures, a good deal of work has been done on the pattern of income distribution and on the incidence of poverty.[6] The broadly general finding of all these studies has been that social policy has effected little redistribution of opportunities and resources, despite the often extravagant claims and considerable fears voiced at the time of passing the relevant measures.

SOCIOLOGICAL EXPLANATIONS OF SOCIAL POLICY

Just as comparative studies of social policy in different countries stimulated the search for a fuller explanation than could be given by the historical approach, so the volume of empirical data on the consequences of specific aspects of welfare legislation emphasized the need to consider measures in relation to the operation of other institutions in society. These might, and often clearly did, influence the effects of any given measure. Taken together, these two factors go a long way towards explaining the quickening of interest in developing a sociological explanation of social policy.

One such explanation, very broad and superficial, but which fitted the observation that social policy had not markedly altered the distribution of life chances between groups in society, was to hand in the shape of Karl Marx's assertion that welfare measures which were developed within the framework of capitalist society could not be expected to effect any basic redistribution.

Marx defined capitalist society as essentially a system of production for profit where the allocation of goods and resources was through the economic market in accordance with effective demand, or the ability to pay. He therefore considered that welfare measures, which allocated goods and services according to need rather than ability to pay, were in fundamental contradiction to capitalism. They would, he argued, have to be wrested from the owning class by working-class agitation and militancy, and even then the owners would grant only such niggardly concessions as would avoid outright revolt by the workers, and would never concede any real redistribution of property or opportunities.

The Marxist explanation, however, is not compatible with the fact that such welfare legislation has not reflected a clearly expressed working-class demand. To cite just three examples: the factory legislation of the nineteenth century, which Marx claimed as a working-class victory, was opposed by sections of the workforce at the time;[7] the introduction of family allowance in 1946 was opposed by some trade unions;[8] and the raising of the school leaving age to sixteen in 1970 had very little support from working-class parents or pupils.

The recognition of a situation as one requiring government intervention, and then framing policies to meet the need defined, is a far more complex process than is suggested by the belief that welfare legislation is solely a response to pressure from the underprivileged. While public unrest might be a factor encouraging recognition of a situation as one for which some legislative action is required, this is by no means invariable. Even where unrest is evident, it is seldom combined with a clearly articulated policy demand. Many measures, like raising the school leaving age, for example, or re-classifying alcoholism as a disease to be treated rather than as moral deviance to be punished, as was done in 1971, are introduced without any public agitation for them at all.

The complexity of social policy processes has been well illustrated in some excellently researched and detailed studies of specific legislative provisions.[9] These meticulous reports make an impressive contrast to the unacceptable superficiality of the Marxist explanation of the role of social policy, but they do not attempt to offer an alternative over-view of the development of social policy as a whole.

SOCIAL POLICY AS AN EGALITARIAN INFLUENCE

Yet some alternative is surely needed, since within the field of social administration there has long been a pronounced tendency to regard welfare policy as being, or meaning to be, aimed at the removal of privilege and the establishment of a more egalitarian social order. This was certainly the view expressed by Aneurin Bevan, the architect of the National Health Service, who declared that while welfare measures were becoming a part of the capitalist system – 'they do not flow from it. They have come in spite of it . . . In claiming them, capitalism proudly displays medals won in the battles it has lost.'[10]

This was also the view of Titmuss, who echoed Marx in contrasting the value of the economic market, where profit and the ability to pay were the determinants, with those of the social market, where need was the criterion for allocation of goods and services. For Titmuss, the development of social policy was best seen as a series of battles to substitute the value of the social market for those of the economic market in one exchange situation after another.[11] Unlike Marx, Titmuss believed such battles could be won and that the nature of capitalism could thus be significantly modified.

Because of the leading role which Titmuss has played in establishing social administration as an academic discipline in this country, his view of social policy as an equalizing force in society has been widely disseminated and very influential for many years. The fact remains, however, that social policy in Britain and elsewhere has effected no radical redistribution over the years, nor has it developed in contradiction to the needs of the economy. This has meant that students of social policy have been caught on the horns of a dilemma. Either they must conclude that all welfare measures are dismal failures because they have not achieved the redistribution of opportunities intended, or they must accept that social policy is not, and never was, in opposition to the economic market and the prevailing social order.

The former view implies that generations of legislators and parliamentary draughtsmen have been utterly incompetent in framing the many instruments of social policy – a patently unsupportable assertion. None the less, the persistence of the belief that welfare measures are attempts at redistribution which have failed has served to dishearten and demoralize many of our social workers and social administrators, reducing both their job satisfaction and their commitment. If the latter view of the complementarity of social welfare measures and the economic market is held, then there is an urgent need to develop the logical connections between social policies and the wider aims of society in which economic considerations continue to be paramount.

SOCIAL POLICY AS AN EXPRESSION OF MORAL DEVELOPMENT

One such attempt is that of Pinker, who rejected Titmuss's idea of opposing social and economic markets and suggested instead a model of 'mercantile collectivism', where social policy was dependent upon the capacity of the economy but served to temper the ruthless individualism of an unchecked free market economy.[12]

Pinker's concept of mercantile collectivism rested on his acceptance of the primacy of economic considerations because, as he pointed out, the enhancement of social welfare must ultimately depend on the efficient production of the goods and services which comprise a satisfactory standard of living. The collective element of the concept was derived by Pinker from his analysis of the moral development of individuals in society. He claimed that individuals today were morally conscious of wider boundaries of obligation than in the past and were more concerned with the welfare of others as well as of themselves. Pinker agreed that the family defined the limits of the strongest feelings of altruism, but argued that there was also a sense of responsibility towards the local community, the nation as a whole, and even, on occasions, to world humanity. As Pinker pointed out, the interests of the family may, and often will, predispose towards a jealous defence of privilege or an attack on others to redress a felt deprivation, thus conflicting with the wider loyalties he mentioned. The fact that people now accept some sacrifice of individual and family interest for the sake of promoting the welfare of the larger collectivity ought, Pinker suggested, '[to] give grounds for optimism regarding the capacity of our moral sentiments'.[13]

A little further in his discussion of welfare, however, Pinker observed that 'the more these sacrifices are required to transcend kinship affiliations, the more likely it is that compulsions and sanctions will be employed by government'.[14] This would indeed seem to be an accurate observation, and surely contradicts the idea that the boundaries of our spontaneous feelings of moral obligation have greatly expanded beyond the family. On the contrary, with greater geographical mobility and the growth of huge impersonal urban areas, it is arguable that the ties with extended kin and with the local community are for most people weaker now than in the past, and that the smaller, privatized family (to use a concept developed by John Goldthorpe in his studies of the affluent worker[15]), so prevalent in today's society, represents a narrower boundary of loyalty than ever before.

None the less, it is a fact that families do make sacrifices for the welfare of others in the nation – people with whom they may have no contact, of whom they may have little knowledge, and for whom they may have little sympathy. These sacrifices are commonly made in response to compulsion and most usually take the form of surrendering a proportion of income in taxation, or limitations on the development and use of the family's own property.

Pinker did not really consider *why* governments should seek to compel such an extension of the boundaries of concern, but in commenting *how*, in a democratic state, individual families are persuaded to accept as justified the compulsion to sacrifice family income and freedom in order to promote the welfare of unknown others, he noted that the acceptability of social policies depends on their having meaning and significance for the citizenry. As it is clear that this meaning and significance could not derive from the individual citizen's emotional commitment to altruistic self-sacrifice on behalf of his fellow man, since compulsion would not then be necessary, some other explanation must be sought.

SOCIAL POLICY AS IDEOLOGICALLY NEUTRAL

For some reason, governments in a wide variety of modern democratic countries decide to impose on their citizens obligations to subordinate self and family interests to the needs of others in the society. One sociological school of thought has argued that it is the logic of technological development which constrains governments, whatever their traditions or political complexions, to institute broadly similar social policies at similar stages of economic growth. This view was held by Harold Wilensky, who made a study of welfare policies in sixty-four countries and concluded that economic development, the age structure of the population, and the age of the social security system, explained 83 per cent of the variance between countries in social security provision. He commented that 'the primacy of an economic level, and its bureaucratic and demographic correlates, is support for a convergence hypothesis; economic growth makes countries with contrasting cultural and political traditions more alike in their strategy for constructing the floor below which no one sinks'.[16]

Certainly Lord Beveridge, in his report on welfare needs made in 1942[17], argued that to have a social security system was neither socialist nor capitalist, but merely common sense. The attempt to remove social policy from the political arena and make it an ideologically neutral correlate of economic advance has not gone unchallenged. An article by two political scientists[18] which refers in its title to 'the sheer futility of the sociological approach to politics' goes on to criticize the evidence on which Wilensky based his assertions. They, in their turn, adduce empirical data to support their contention that political ideologies can be seen to be the main determinant of what they consider to be very different levels of welfare provision in countries at roughly the same economic level. It is possible to quarrel with their interpretation of their data, and certainly they have not proved that ideological considerations are the main, let alone the only, determinant of welfare policies. They have, however, given us a cogent and timely reminder that, even if it is only common sense for advanced societies to develop systems of welfare, and even if this may be seen to have happened in industrial countries across the world, there is still room for moral choice about the level and emphasis of welfare provision – in other words, there is still room for politics, in any complete explanation of the development of social policies.

SOCIAL POLICY AND ECONOMIC RATIONALITY

The argument advanced in this book, illustrated by a study of welfare provisions for handicapped people in Britain, attempts to reconcile the view that social policy is the logical outcome of economic development with the continuing existence of moral or political choice.

Basically, this argument is that rationality is a dominant, even necessary, value in all highly industrial societies. The citizenry is from a very young age trained to assess the worth of an action or a given line of conduct by its outcome, rather than by whether or not it conforms to traditional customs or beliefs. This, of course, is not a new point about value systems in industrial society. It has been argued by many, including notably Max Weber.[19] If, however, individuals and governments judge actions by their outcome, these must be susceptible of measurement in an objectively verifiable manner, even when the outcome is a quality such as good health or welfare. This normally means measuring the outcome in materialistic or economic terms. Hence economic rationality, it is contended here, has become the criterion by which to judge when government intervention to compel individual and family sacrifice in order to promote the welfare of certain other groups is justified. Where such intervention is expected to result not only in enhancing the well-being of the immediate beneficiaries of the welfare measure but also in conferring a net benefit on society as a whole, such action is accepted as economically rational and can command the commitment of collective resources.

In the closely integrated modern industrial state, the truth of the old saw that no man is an island unto himself has become increasingly evident, and has led to the recognition of an increasing number of situations, such as childhood, unemployment, sickness and homelessness, as being appropriate areas for collective provision, for the sake of the well-being of society as a whole.

SOCIAL POLICY AND POLITICAL CHOICE

In producing evidence of the ways in which intervention to promote welfare in one area of society can have indirect beneficial consequences for a much larger group than those singled out for direct benefit, the social sciences have played a significant role. Much sociological effort is spent in analysing the inter-dependence of institutions and groups in society, and in tracing the processes by which change in one area works its way through the social structure and affects a wide range of institutional relationships. In economics, a major activity is assessing the repercussions of various forms of economic intervention. Psychology and political science also make their contributions to our understanding of individual behaviour and the processes of democratic government. Despite the growing explanatory power of the social sciences, however, they lack precise predictive ability, and it is in the nature of the social sciences, with the multiplicity of variables with which they are concerned, many of them not susceptible to control or systematic manipulation, that precision in prediction will remain a chimera. This means that there will always be scope for argument as to what the consequences of any particular action, or lack of action, will be, and therefore scope for political choice as to which set of probabilities is the more attractive. The overriding importance of the economic consequences of any proposed welfare measure is not, and has not been for many years, a matter of political debate.

It is the common emphasis on rationality apparent in advanced industrial societies, coupled with the interdependence of all sections of the community resulting from the increasing specialization of labour which accompanies technological development, which has resulted in the identification of similar areas for collective welfare provision in the various countries. The calculation, in objective material terms, of the consequences of action or inaction in certain commonly encountered human situations has encouraged the development of broadly similar social policies. Some diversity in provision is, however, inevitable, because the calculation of the costs and benefits of any line of action is not precise but a matter for argument. Even the component factors to be included in a particular welfare equation are often a matter for fierce debate, as well as the economic values attaching to them.

Political preferences as to where to draw the line between factors to be included or excluded in the equation, and where the benefit of the doubt will lie in calculating costs and benefits, can be very important. Social policy in countries which have experienced a long and continuous record of political bias in one direction may evolve a noticeably different emphasis from that of countries without such a sustained bias, or, more particularly, with a consistent but opposing bias. Economic rationality dictates that the sums must be done, but not the answers.

ECONOMIC RATIONALITY AND THE SOCIAL RESPONSE TO HANDICAP

The presentation and discussion of social policies concerning handicapped people given earlier in this book illustrate the paramount influence of considerations of economic rationality in the formulation and operation of welfare measures for disabled people. These considerations have been seen to influence not only the type and level of services developed but also, more fundamentally, public attitudes towards disability and disabled people. The emphasis on the economic prosperity of the nation encourages a concentration on individual achievement, materialistic aspirations and competitive effort in work and play, with the inevitable corollary that anyone with a disability which handicaps him in the race for success is correspondingly devalued.

However compassionate the social response to handicap may be, the fact that it is informed by considerations of economic rationality means that the social values which esteem competent independence have never been seriously challenged, so that disability continues to carry a social stigma.

Moreover, which ever political party has been in power, the overall trend of social policy towards disabled people has varied only within the narrow limits set by the common application of the criterion of economic rationality. Some differences in timing and emphasis of measures due to political preference has been apparent, and these differences may have had significant consequences for some individual handicapped men, women or children. Nevertheless, whatever the complexion of the government, social policies in respect of disabled people have only underlined the value of economic rationality by being advanced, argued and accepted in terms of the financial costs and benefits to the society as a whole.

Some may find very distasteful the notion that rational economic calculations underly the development of welfare, and may wish to pursue the creation of the good society in which humanitarian concerns take precedence over economic considerations. But there has never been, and is not now, agreement over what constitutes a morally good society. Attempts to define it in terms of moral absolutes, or natural law, or maximization of happiness, have all been found wanting in the past as a guide to appropriate state action to promote welfare. Moreover, societies based on a conviction of moral righteousness have often proved extremely intolerant of those who could not share the prevailing view of what was right and good.

The fact that economic rationality is the fundamental criterion of action need not imply a callous indifference to the welfare of the weak or unfortunate while the strong amass their fortunes. On the contrary, in encouraging a concentration on hard facts, such as those yielded by various poverty surveys, household surveys, housing enquiries, health and disability statistics, it has resulted in a readier and more embracing perception of collective responsibility for welfare. There are disadvantages in a calculative approach to welfare, of course, and these have been indicated and discussed in relation to social provision for handicapped people. None the less, the principle of economic rationality can still be seen to offer the best hope of peaceful piecemeal improvements in the lives of the majority of the people, including handicapped people.

NOTES AND REFERENCES

1. Education (Provision of Meals) Act 1906.
2. Education (Administrative Provisions) Act 1907.
3. See, for example, P. HALL, H. LAND, R. PARKER AND A. WEBB, *Change, Choice and Conflict*, Heinemann, London (1975); R. MISHRA, *Society and Social Policy*, Macmillan, London (1977); and R. PINKER, *The Idea of Welfare*, Heinemann, London (1979).
4. For a review of studies in this field see W. TYLER, *The Sociology of Educational Inequality*, Methuen, London (1977).
5. DHSS, *Inequalities in Health*, DHSS (1980) (Chairman: Sir Douglas Black).
6. D. WEDDERBURN (ed.) *Poverty, Inequality and Class Structure*, Cambridge University Press (1974).
7. There was, for example, working–class opposition to legislation limiting the working hours of women and children – see S. AND B. WEBB, 'Problems of Modern Industry', in R. C. K. ENSOR (ed.) *Modern Socialism*, Harper & Bros., London (1910).
8. P. HALL *et. al.*, *op. cit.*
9. *Ibid.*
10. A. BEVAN, *In Place of Fear*, Heinemann, London (1952), p. 74.
11. This view is implicit in much of Titmuss's work but is given clearest expression in R. TITMUSS, *Commitment to Welfare*, Allen & Unwin, London (1962); and R. TITMUSS, *The Gift Relationship*, Allen & Unwin, London (1970).
12. R. PINKER, *op. cit.*
13. *Ibid.*, p. 38
14. *Ibid.*, p. 41.
15. J. GOLDTHORPE, D. LOCKWOOD, F. BECHOFER AND J. PLATT, *The Affluent Worker*, Cambridge University Press (1968).
16. H. WILENSKY, *The Welfare State and Equality*, University of California Press, Berkeley (1975).
17. *Report on Social Insurance and Allied Services*, Cmnd 6404, HMSO (1942) (Chairman: Sir William Beveridge).
18. F. G. CASTLES AND R. D. MCKINLAY, 'Public Welfare Provision, Scandinavia, and the Sheer Futility of the Sociological

Approach to Politics', *British Journal of Political Science*, Vol. 9, April 1979.

19. MAX WEBER, *The Protestant Ethic and the Spirit of Capitalism*, George Allen & Unwin, London (1930).

Part four
DOCUMENTS

Document one
INTEGRATION IN EDUCATION

Section 10 of the Education Act 1976 was intended to replace section 33 of the Education Act 1944, and would have given handicapped children the right to attend ordinary schools unless such a course was quite impracticable. The date on which the new section would come into force was, however, left to the discretion of the Secretary of State for Education. The provision had not been implemented when there was a change of government in 1979, and the incoming administration announced the intention of leaving section 10 ineffective.
Section 10 of the Education Act 1976 is given below.

Pupils requiring special educational treatment.
(10)(1) For section 33(2) of the Education Act 1944 there shall be substituted –

'(2) The arrangements made by a local education authority for the special educational treatment of pupils of any such category shall, subject to subsection (2A) of this section, provide for the education of the pupils in county or voluntary schools.
(2A) Where the education of the pupils in such schools as aforesaid –
(*a*) is impracticable or incompatible with the provision of efficient instruction in the schools: or
(*b*) would involve unreasonable public expenditure,
the arrangements may provide for the education of the pupils in special schools appropriate to the category to which the pupils belong or in schools not maintained by a local education authority and for the time being notified by the Secretary of State to the authority as in his opinion suitable for the purpose.'

From: Education Act 1976

Document two
SPECIAL NEEDS IN EDUCATION

In 1980 the government produced its proposals for implementing the recommendations of the Warnock Report.* Extracts from these proposals† are given below.

INTEGRATION

35. There are legitimate differences of view over where and how a child with special educational needs is best educated. The Government takes as its starting point the principle that children and young people who have such needs should be educated in association with those who do not. But this principle must always be applied so as not to frustrate the aim of giving the child or student, within the limits of what is practicable, the greatest possible opportunity to benefit from the education process. The right placement for a child with a serious disability can only be properly determined after careful assessment of his needs by competent professionals and in close consultation with his parents. For some children with special needs association, or full association, with other children is the wrong solution and to impose it would be unfair to the child, his parents, other children and the taxpayer. In such a case the arguments for full association must give way to other arguments which are more valid in that case.

36. Accordingly the Government does not propose to bring into force section 10 of the Education Act 1976. To do so would entail perpetuating the concept of categories of disability, because the section builds on the provision in the Education Act 1944 which incorporates that concept. But section 10 is open to more general objections. It gives no opportunity to the expression of parental preference. It is too narrowly concerned with merely placing a handicapped pupil in an ordinary school, which does not by itself guarantee that the child will be educated in association with chil-

* *Special Educational Needs, Report of the Committee of Enquiry into the Education of Handicapped Children and Young People*, Cmnd 7212, HMSO, London (1978). (Chairman: Mrs Mary Warnock.)

† DES *Special Needs in Education*, Cmnd 7996, HMSO, London (1980).

dren who are not handicapped. Above all, it does not take sufficient account of the fact that every child has his own educational needs. Many handicapped children would stand less chance of having their needs met if they were obliged to attend the ordinary schools with their present facilities and resources. Yet in present economic circumstances there is no possibility of finding the massive additional resources for the education and health services which would be required to enable every ordinary school to provide an adequate education for children with serious educational difficulties, without thereby providing a less than adequate education for the other pupils.

37. The Government intends that the process of planned and sensible integration of handicapped children into ordinary schools should continue. However, children with serious difficulties must not be obliged to attend ordinary schools if these cannot fully provide for their needs. In the Government's view, it will continue to be necessary to provide places in special schools and classes, and to make other special arrangements, e.g. through education at home or in hospital, for some of the most seriously handicapped children.

38. The development of the education service will need to take place within the financial limits set by the public expenditure plans which the Government has announced. Present arrangements for handicapped persons make relatively modest calls on local authority budgets. In the Government's view, authorities will be able to give progressively fuller expression to the new approach outlined in this White Paper by the gradual redeployment of resources. The good practice already achieved by some authorities provides a substantial base on which to build. The Secretaries of State will also be ready to advise authorities about meeting their proposed new responsibilities.

III THE GOVERNMENT'S PROPOSALS

39. In accordance with the approach outlined in Section II, the Government proposes legislation which will do away with the present system of special educational treatment for children ascertained as belonging to a category of handicap. Instead it proposes in this area to base the duties and powers of LEAs and schools, and the rights and duties of parents, on the concept that certain children have special educational needs. A minority of such children will, as the Warnock Committee recommended, be the subject of a formal record, on the basis of which the LEA, in the interest of the child, will take special steps in regard to his education and keep his progress under regular formal review. But most such children will be educated without the formality of a record. It is likely that, at least initially, 'recorded' children will roughly correspond to those who at present have been ascertained as requiring special educational treatment. It will be for the LEA to decide whether a child's needs are such that he ought to be 'recorded'; and it will not be able to decide that he should,

except on the basis of a multi-professional assessment carried out in accordance with rules prescribed by the Secretary of State.

DEFINITION OF SPECIAL EDUCATIONAL NEEDS

40. The Government envisages a broad definition of special educational needs, to include those needs which are attributable to a physical, sensory, or mental disability or an emotional or behavioural disorder and which call for special provision in respect of such matters as the location, content, timing, or method of education, and any other needs which are similar in their effect. Within its general duty to secure a sufficiency of schools for its area the LEA will have a duty to have regard to the need to secure adequate provision for pupils with special educational needs, instead of, as at present, for pupils who require special educational treatment because they fall into a defined category of handicap.

INTEGRATION: STATEMENT OF PRINCIPLE

41. The Government proposes that a child with special educational needs who is not a 'recorded' child should normally be educated in an ordinary school; and that a 'recorded' child shall also, wherever this is reasonable and practicable, be so educated. Accordingly the proposed legislation will provide that a child with special educational needs shall be educated with children without such needs, provided that the arrangements are capable of meeting his needs, are compatible with the efficient education of the children with whom he is to be educated, and with the efficient use of public resources, and take proper account of the wishes of his parents. This provision will replace section 10 of the 1976 Education Act.

SPECIAL AND INDEPENDENT SCHOOLS

42. The adoption, on this basis, of the principle of integration makes it necessary to ensure that where a 'recorded' child cannot be educated at an ordinary school, alternative arrangements can be made available. The Government therefore proposes to retain the present system of maintained and non-maintained special schools whose arrangements are subject to the approval of the Secretary of State; and to augment it by a new category of independent schools which will be approved by the Secretary of State as suitable for the admission of 'recorded' children. As in the case of the special schools, approval will be conditional on the school's compliance with regulations governing its general conduct, staffing, premises and educational standards. The Secretary of State will maintain a list of all independent schools suitable for the admission of 'recorded' children. A LEA will not normally be allowed to place a 'recorded' child in an independent school which is not on this list.

43. The Government is consulting non-maintained special schools about alterations to the composition of their governing bodies to bring them into line with the requirements for the governing bodies of maintained special schools under the Education Act 1980. The Government has also

considered whether independent schools approved for the education of 'recorded' children should, as the Warnock Committee recommended, be required to have governing bodies. The Government has decided that such a requirement would be neither fair nor practicable. Many independent schools are commercial enterprises and their proprietors could not reasonably be expected to surrender control to persons whom they did not themselves appoint. The Government considers that the power to approve an independent school for the admission of 'recorded' children adequately protects the public interest. But it will encourage such schools to appoint advisory committees to help them discharge their highly specialised task.

44. Under the present law the Secretary of State has to approve the establishment of a new special school. But a LEA does not need his approval for closing a special school which it maintains. The Government proposes that LEAs should be required to afford an opportunity to the parents of children attending the school and to other interested parties to make representations about a proposal to close such a school; and to seek the Secretary of State's approval to closure.

IDENTIFICATION OF CHILDREN WITH SPECIAL EDUCATIONAL NEEDS

45. The present duty of LEAs to discover children requiring special educational treatment can in practice be fully discharged only in respect of children registered at a school maintained by the LEA. The LEA is in no position to inform itself of the potential educational problems of every child in its area who is under compulsory school age or attends an independent school. Under the proposed new legislation a LEA will only be required, in relation to children between the ages of two and five who are not receiving education in a school maintained by the LEA and children attending independent schools, to follow up cases which come to its notice (e.g. through the parents or a health visitor) of any child whose special educational needs might justify his being 'recorded'; in relation to pupils of any age in a school maintained by the LEA there will be a duty either on the school or on the LEA to identify all children with special educational needs, and not only those who should be 'recorded'. Once a child with special needs has been identified, there will be a duty on the LEA or school to meet his needs in accordance with the arrangements set out in paragraph 47 below.

46. Since it is sometimes desirable to tackle special educational needs when children are under two years of age, it is proposed to empower LEAs to 'record' such children and to arrange for their education. But this power will be exercised only with the consent of the parents.

MEETING SPECIAL EDUCATIONAL NEEDS

47. In the case of the ordinary schools which it maintains, the LEA will be required, in consultation with school governors and head teachers in the case of county and voluntary schools, to keep under review the

arrangements made in these schools for meeting the special educational needs of the pupils. Each county and voluntary school, in accordance with the respective responsibilities of the governors, the head teacher and the LEA, will be under a duty to meet the special needs of its pupils having regard to the resources available to the school, including the advisory and support services provided by the LEA and by the health and personal social services. Where a school considers that it cannot meet the special needs of a pupil, it will be required to inform the LEA, who must then consider, in consultation with the school and, as appropriate, the parents, whether the child's needs are best met by arrangements under which he remains at the school or by other arrangements. In the case of nursery schools it will be for the LEA to ensure that special educational needs are met.

48. The action taken in the case of children who are not 'recorded' will in principle be similar to what happens now when either the school or the LEA consider that a child should not attend a particular school. It will be for the LEA to control, direct and adjust its resources as at present so that they can be used to the best advantage of the schools and their pupils. But it will be even more necessary for the LEA to advise schools on good practice and the most effective use of resources, for schools to be ready to share their expertise with each other, and for the LEA and the governors to work closely together for their common purpose. The Government believes that, with goodwill, it will seldom prove necessary for either the LEA or the governors to ask the Secretary of State to settle differences which they have been unable to resolve locally.

49. The new status of 'recorded' children will place fresh responsibilities on the ordinary schools in which many such children are, and will be, educated. The success and commitment with which many schools already tackle the often complex special needs of certain of their pupils while still meeting the needs of all the others, points the way to the effective discharge of these new responsibilities.

50. Where the child is not 'recorded', the arrangements governing the choice of school and the school attendance procedures established by the Education Act 1980 will apply. For 'recorded' children new arrangements are proposed: these are set out in paragraph 58 below.

POST 16

51. As a child with special educational needs reaches the end of compulsory schooling his parents–no less than other parents–are faced with important decisions about his education and training. The Government strongly endorses the recommendations of the Warnock Committee on careers education and guidance during the later years of compulsory schooling, although it accepts that the priority given to this aspect of the curriculum must be considered alongside other pressures on it. As young people in school approach school leaving age, the Careers Service as part of its general function has an important role to play, in providing voca-

tional guidance and advice on employment, further education and training to handicapped young people, and working closely with careers teachers. The possibilities for continued education and vocational training will depend to a considerable extent on the nature and degree of the special educational needs of the individual child. The Government believes that the range of opportunities should, within the limits of what is practicable, be as comprehensive for young people with special educational needs as for others. Some of them will wish to pursue courses leading to public examinations; those at ordinary schools may be able to continue their studies in accordance with an authority's normal arrangements. Some pupils at special schools, where suitable arrangements can be made, should also be enabled to stay on after the age of 16 or join sixth-forms or sixth-form colleges if they would benefit from doing so. For others, however, it will be more beneficial to leave school and seek education or training in another setting. These young people should be able to look to the further education system for the help they need.

52. It is a weakness of the law governing further education that it makes no specific reference to the needs of handicapped students. The Government recognises the need to clarify the law in the interest of students with special educational needs. But this will need to be done as part of a wider review of the legal framework governing further education on which the Secretaries of State are initiating consultations with the local authority associations and will in due course consult more widely. Meanwhile a growing number of LEAs and colleges are meeting the special needs of students. Some colleges have shown commendable enterprise in developing courses suited to students with special educational needs along the lines recommended by the Warnock Committee and some progress has been made in adapting college accommodation to give easier access to courses for students with physical handicaps. Large-scale expansion of such opportunities will not be possible in present economic circumstances. But the Government hopes that LEAs will continue to examine, both locally and regionally, ways to increase the scale and variety of provision, taking into account the important contribution of the voluntary organisations active in this field.

53. The Government does not accept the recommendation of the Warnock Committee that LEAs should become responsible for a specific educational element in adult training and day centres. This is not practicable. These centres will function efficiently only if they are run under a single direction. But there should be increasing co-operation between education and social services departments over the educational aspects of the work, including the various ways in which further education teachers and facilities can best make their contribution in each situation.

RECORDING

54. For children whose special educational needs call for formal recording by the LEA, the Government proposes the following arrangements.

As was explained in paragraph 39 above, the decision to 'record' a child will lie with the LEA. It is the Government's intention that a LEA should not 'record' a child if his special educational needs can be met by attendance at the ordinary schools maintained by the LEA without the need of systematic annual review by the LEA. The LEA will first have to decide whether there is a prima facie case for recording which is sufficiently strong to justify the multi-professional assessment which will be a prerequisite of recording. It will take this preliminary decision in the light of information which it receives about the child, e.g. from his parents or school. The parents of a child aged two or over will have the right to request a multi-professional assessment, and the LEA will have to meet that request unless it is unreasonable.

55. The exact nature of the multi-professional assessment will depend on the circumstances of each case. But the Secretary of State will prescribe broad rules which will govern the assessment. These will include the requirement that the medical, psychological and pedagogic aspects must each be covered by a qualified professional person. If the child is two or over, the parents will be required to submit him for the examinations involved in the assessment and will have the right to attend them.

56. The LEA will have to consider the assessment and also take into account any relevant reports or other information about the child. In particular it will have to consider any views expressed by the parents. If it decides that the child should be 'recorded', the record will be in a form prescribed by the Secretary of State and will have two parts. The first will be a description of the child's special educational needs stemming from the multi-professional assessment and other information received by the LEA; the second part will set out the educational arrangements which the LEA proposes to make to meet these needs: in making the proposal in the second part the LEA will have to have regard to the description of special needs in the first.

57. The Government agrees with the widely-held view that it would be wrong to require full disclosure to parents of the professional reports lying behind the record. Professional reports must remain confidential if they are to give the LEA fully and frankly the information it needs in assessing and meeting special educational needs. Parents have an absolute right to know how the LEA judges their child's educational needs in the light of the multi-professional assessment and the Government acknowledges this. It proposes that the LEA will have to give the parents an opportunity to see the record which it proposes to make in respect of their child, and will have to consider any comments they make on the record. If the parents argue that their child should not be 'recorded' and the LEA does not accept this, the parents will have the right to refer to an appeals committee, in accordance with the provisions set out below, the question of which school should provide for the child. Parents will similarly have the right to take their case to an appeals committee if the LEA decides that their child should not be 'recorded', but they wish him

to be. In such cases the parents will have a right to be informed of the LEA's reasons for its decision not to 'record' the child.

APPEALS

58. Once the LEA has made a record, it will have a duty to act in accordance with the second part of the record, unless it is satisfied that the parents are making adequate arrangements. The LEA will normally carry out this duty by arranging to place the child in a particular school. This may be an ordinary school, possibly in a special class or unit of the school; a special school; or an independent school approved for the admission of 'recorded' children. The placement will require the consent of the parents if the child is below compulsory school age. If the child is of compulsory school age and the parents dispute the placement, they will have the right to bring the matter before a LEA appeals committee established by the Education Act 1980. But in this class of case, since the circumstances may be very special and the decision may have substantial resource implications, the committee's findings will not be binding on the LEA but will be in the nature of a recommendation to it. This difference in the committee's function will affect its operation. For example it will have to be able to consider the child's record and to comment on its contents. But subject to this, the Government intends the provisions governing this part of the committee's work to be as close as possible to those which govern its other work.

59. If the committee recommends the LEA to reconsider the proposed placement, the LEA will be under a duty to do so. If it confirms its earlier decision on placement, or if the committee's recommendation endorses that placement, the parents will have the right to appeal to the Secretary of State, who will be empowered to cancel or amend the record, after consulting the LEA.

From: *Special Needs in Education*, Cmnd 7996, HMSO, London (1980).

Document three
THE CHRONICALLY SICK AND DISABLED PERSONS ACT 1970

The Chronically Sick and Disabled Persons Act 1970 is relevant to so many of the issues concerning the welfare of disabled people that it is given in full below.

Chronically Sick and Disabled Persons Act 1970
(1970 c. 44)

ARRANGEMENT OF SECTIONS

An Act to make further provision with respect to the welfare of chronically sick and disabled persons; and for connected purposes.
[29th May 1970]

General Note

This Act makes further provision with respect to the welfare of chronically sick and disabled persons.

S. 1 imposes on local authorities a duty to inform themselves as to the need for and existence of welfare services. S. 2 concerns the provision of welfare services and s. 3 the duties of housing authorities. S. 4 deals with access to, and facilities at, premises open to the public. S. 5 relates to the provision of public sanitary conveniences. S. 6 concerns the provision of sanitary conveniences at certain premises open to the public. S. 7 provides for signs at buildings complying with ss. 4–6. S. 8 deals with access to, and facilities at, university and school buildings. S. 9 concerns the central advisory committee on war pensions, s. 10 Housing Advisory Committees, s. 11 the National Insurance Advisory Committee, s. 12 the Industrial Injuries Advisory Council, s. 13 the Youth Employment Service and s. 14 miscellaneous advisory committees. S. 15 provides for the co-option of chronically sick or disabled persons to local authority committees and s. 16 specifies the duties of the national advisory council established under s. 17 of the Disabled Persons (Employment) Act 1944. S. 17 provides for the separation of younger from older hospital patients, s. 18 concerns information as to accommodation of younger with older persons under Part III of the National Assistance Act 1948 and s. 19 deals with the provision of information relating to chiropody services. S. 20 concerns the use of invalid carriages on highways and s. 21 provides that badges shall be issued for display on motor vehicles used by disabled persons. S. 22 relates to an annual report on research and development work. S. 23 concerns war pensions appeals. S. 24 deals with the institute of hearing research. S. 25 makes provision for special educational treatment for the deaf-blind and s. 26 for children suffering from acute dyslexia. S. 28 empowers the Secretary of State to make regulations defining certain expressions and s. 29 contains short title, extent and commencement.

The Act, which does not apply to Northern Ireland, except as expressly provided by ss. 9, 14, 23, applies to Scotland with the exception of ss. 1–2. The Act received the Royal Assent on May 29, 1970, and comes into force as follows: Ss. 1, 21, on a date to be appointed, ss. 4–8 on November 29, 1970, and the remainder on August 29, 1970.

For definitions, see s. 25.

For parliamentary debates, see H.L. Vol. 309, cols. 239, 1115; Vol. 310, cols. 837, 1085; H.C. Vol. 792, col. 1851; Vol. 798, col. 831; Vol. 801, col. 2004.

SCOTLAND

The Act (except ss. 1, 2) does not apply to Scotland (s. 26 (2)).

Welfare and Housing

INFORMATION AS TO NEED FOR AND EXISTENCE OF WELFARE SERVICES

1.–(1) It shall be the duty of every local authority having functions under section 29 of the National Assistance Act 1948 to inform themselves of the number of persons to whom that section applies within their area and of the need for the making by the authority of arrangements under that section for such persons.

(2) Every such local authority –

(*a*) shall cause to be published from time to time at such times and in such manner as they consider appropriate general information as to the services provided under arrangements made by the authority under the said section 29 which are for the time being available in their area; and

(*b*) shall ensure that any such person as aforesaid who uses any of those services is informed of any other of those services which in the opinion of the authority is relevant to his needs.

(3) This section shall come into operation on such date as the Secretary of State may by order made by statutory instrument appoint.

PROVISION OF WELFARE SERVICES

2.–(1) Where a local authority having functions under section 29 of the National Assistance Act 1948 are satisfied in the case of any person to whom that section applies who is ordinarily resident in their area that it is necessary in order to meet the needs of that person for that authority to make arrangements for all or any of the following matters, namely–

(*a*) the provision of practical assistance for that person in his home;

(*b*) the provision for that person of, or assistance to that person in obtaining, wireless, television, library or similar recreational facilities;

(*c*) the provision for that person of lectures, games, outings or other recreational facilities outside his home or assistance to that person in taking advantage of educational facilities available to him;

(*d*) the provision for that person of facilities for, or assistance in, travelling to and from his home for the purpose of participating in any services provided under arrangements made by the authority under the said section 29 or, with the approval of the authority, in any services provided otherwise than as aforesaid which are similar to services which could be provided under such arrangements;

(*e*) the provision of assistance for that person in arranging for the carrying out of any works of adaptation in his home or the provision of any additional facilities designed to secure his greater safety, comfort or convenience;

(*f*) facilitating the taking of holidays by that person, whether at holiday homes or otherwise and whether provided under arrangements made by the authority or otherwise;

(*g*) the provision of meals for that person whether in his home or elsewhere;

(*h*) the provision for that person of, or assistance to that person in obtaining, a telephone and any special equipment necessary to enable him to use a telephone,

then, notwithstanding anything in any scheme made by the authority under the said section 29, but subject to the provisions of section 35 (2) of that Act (which requires local authorities to exercise their functions under Part III of that Act under the general guidance of the Secretary of State and in accordance with the provisions of any regulations made for the purpose), it shall be the duty of that authority to make those arrangements in exercise of their functions under the said section 29.

(2) Without prejudice to the said section 35 (2), subsection (3) of the said section 29 (which requires any arrangements made by a local authority under that section to be carried into effect in accordance with a scheme made thereunder) shall not apply–

(*a*) to any arrangements made in pursuance of subsection (1) of this section; or (*b*) in the case of a local authority who have made such a scheme, to any arrangements made by virtue of subsection (1) of the said section 29 in addition to those required or authorised by the scheme which are so made with the approval of the Secretary of State.

DUTIES OF HOUSING AUTHORITIES

3.–(1) Every local authority for the purposes of Part V of the Housing Act 1957 in discharging their duty under section 91 of that Act to consider housing conditions in their district and the needs of the district with respect to the provision of further housing accommodation shall have regard to the special needs of chronically sick or disabled persons; and any proposals prepared and submitted to the Minister by the authority under that section for the provision of new houses shall distinguish any houses which the authority propose to provide which make special provision for the needs of such persons.

(2) In the application of this section to Scotland for the words 'Part V of the Housing Act 1957', '91' and 'Minister' there shall be substituted respectively the words 'Part VII of the Housing (Scotland) Act 1966', '137' and 'Secretary of State'.

Premises open to public

ACCESS TO, AND FACILITIES AT, PREMISES OPEN TO THE PUBLIC

4.–(1) Any person undertaking the provision of any building or premises to which the public are to be admitted, whether on payment or otherwise, shall, in the means of access both to and within the building or premises, and in the parking facilities and sanitary conveniences to be available (if any), make provision, in so far as it is in the circumstances both practicable and reasonable, for the needs of members of the public visiting the building or premises who are disabled.

(2) This section shall not apply to any building or premises intended for purposes mentioned in subsection (2) of section 8 of this Act.

PROVISION OF PUBLIC SANITARY CONVENIENCES

5.–(1) Where any local authority undertake the provision of a public sanitary convenience, it shall be the duty of the authority, in doing so, to make provision, in so far as it is in the circumstances both practicable and reasonable, for the needs of disabled persons.

(2) Any local authority which in any public sanitary convenience provided by them make or have made provision for the needs of disabled persons shall take such steps as may be reasonable, by sign-posts or similar notices, to indicate the whereabouts of the convenience.

(3) In this section "local authority" means a local authority within the meaning of the Local Government Act 1933 or the Local Government (Scotland) Act 1947 and any joint board or joint committee of which all the constituent authorities are local authorities within the meaning of either of those Acts.

PROVISION OF SANITARY CONVENIENCES AT CERTAIN PREMISES OPEN TO THE PUBLIC

6.–(1) Any person upon whom a notice is served with respect to any premises under section 89 of the Public Health Act 1936 (which empowers local authorities by notice to make requirements as to the provision and maintenance of sanitary conveniences for the use of persons frequenting certain premises used for the accommodation, refreshment or entertainment of members of the public) shall in complying with that notice make provision, in so far as it is in the circumstances both practicable and reasonable, for the needs of persons frequenting those premises who are disabled.

(2) The owner of a building, who has been ordered under section 11 (4) of the Building (Scotland) Act 1959 to make the building conform to a provision of building standards regulations make under section 3 of that Act requiring the provision of suitable and sufficient sanitary conveniences therein, shall in complying with that order made provision, in so far as it is in the circumstances both practicable and reasonable, for the needs of persons frequenting that building who are disabled.

SIGNS AT BUILDINGS COMPLYING WITH SS. 4–6

7.–(1) Where any provision required by or under section 4, 5 or 6 of this Act is made at a building in compliance with that section, a notice or sign indicating that provision is made for the disabled shall be displayed outside the building or so as to be visible from outside it.

(2) This section applies to a sanitary convenience provided elsewhere than in a building, and not itself being a building, as it applies to a building.

University and school buildings

ACCESS TO, AND FACILITIES AT, UNIVERSITY AND SCHOOL BUILDINGS

8.–(1) Any person undertaking the provision of a building intended for purposes mentioned in subsection (2) below shall, in the means of access both to and within the building, and in the parking facilities and sanitary conveniences to be available (if any), make provision, in so far as it is in the circumstances both practicable and reasonable, for the needs of persons using the building who are disabled.

(2) The purposes referred to in subsection (1) above are the purposes of any of the following:

(*a*) universities, university colleges and colleges, schools and halls of universities;

(*b*) schools within the meaning of the Education Act 1944, teacher training colleges maintained by local education authorities in England or Wales and other institutions providing further education pursuant to a scheme under section 42 of that Act;

(*c*) educational establishments within the meaning of the Education (Scotland) Act 1962.

CENTRAL ADVISORY COMMITTEE ON WAR PENSIONS

9.–(1) The Secretary of State shall ensure that the central advisory committee constituted under section 3 of the War Pensions Act 1921 includes the chairmen of not less than twelve of the committees established by schemes under section 1 of that Act and includes at least one war disabled pensioner, and shall cause that central advisory committee to be convened at least once in every year.

(2) This section extends to Northern Ireland.

HOUSING ADVISORY COMMITTEES

10. In the appointment of persons to be members of the Central Housing Advisory Committee set up under section 143 of the Housing Act 1957 or of the Scottish Housing Advisory Committee set up under section 167 of the Housing (Scotland) Act 1966, regard shall be had to the desirability of that Committee's including one or more persons with knowledge of the problems involved in housing the chronically sick and disabled and to the person or persons with that knowledge being or including a chronically sick or disabled person or persons.

NATIONAL INSURANCE ADVISORY COMMITTEE

11. The National Insurance Advisory Committee shall include at least one person with experience of work among and of the needs of the chronically sick and disabled and in selecting any such person regard shall be had to the desirability of having a chronically sick or disabled person.

INDUSTRIAL INJURIES ADVISORY COUNCIL

12. The Industrial Injuries Advisory Council shall include at least one person with experience of work among and of the needs of the chronically sick and disabled and in selecting any such person regard shall be had to the desirability of having a chronically sick or disabled person.

YOUTH EMPLOYMENT SERVICE

13.–(1) Without prejudice to any other arrangements that may be made by the Secretary of State, the Central Youth Employment Executive shall include at least one person with special responsibility for the employment of young disabled persons.

(2) In the appointment of persons to be members of any of the bodies constituted in pursuance of section 8 (1) of the Employment and Training Act 1948 (that is to say, the National Youth Employment Council and the Advisory Committees on Youth Employment for Scotland and Wales respectively) regard shall be had to the desirability of the body in question including one or more persons with experience of work among, and the special needs of, young disabled persons and to the person or persons with that experience being or including a disabled person or persons.

MISCELLANEOUS ADVISORY COMMITTEES

14.–(1) In the appointment of persons to be members of any of the following advisory committees or councils, that is to say, the Transport Users' Consultative Committees, the Gas Consultative Councils, the Electricity Consultative Councils, the Post Office Users' Councils and the Domestic Coal Consumers' Council, regard shall be had to the desirability of the committee or council in question including one or more persons with experience of work among, and the special needs of, disabled persons and to the person or persons with that experience being or including a disabled person or persons.

(2) In this section the reference to the Post Office Users' Councils is a reference to the Councils established under section 14 of the Post Office Act 1969, and in relation to those Councils this section shall extend to Northern Ireland.

CO-OPTION OF CHRONICALLY SICK OR DISABLED PERSONS TO LOCAL AUTHORITY COMMITTEES

15. Where a local authority within the meaning of the Local Government Act 1933 or the Local Government (Scotland) Act 1947 appoint a committee of the authority under any enactment, and the members of the committee include or may include persons who are not members of the authority, then in considering the appointment to the committee of such persons regard shall be had, if the committee is concerned with matters in which the chronically sick or disabled have special needs, to the desirability of appointing to the committee persons with experience of work among and of the needs of the chronically sick and disabled, and to the person or persons with that experience being or including a chronically sick or disabled person or persons.

DUTIES OF NATIONAL ADVISORY COUNCIL UNDER DISABLED PERSONS (EMPLOYMENT) ACT 1944

16. The duties of the national advisory council established under section 17 (1) (*a*) of the Disabled Persons (Employment) Act 1944 shall include in particular the duty of giving to the Secretary of State such advice as appears to the council to be necessary on the training of persons concerned with–

(*a*) placing disabled persons in employment; or

(*b*) training disabled persons for employment.

Provisions with respect to persons under 65

SEPARATION OF YOUNGER FROM OLDER PATIENTS

17.–(1) Every Board constituted under section 11 of the National Health Service Act 1946 (that is to say, every Regional Hospital Board and every Board of Governors of a teaching hospital) and every Regional Hospital Board constituted under section 11 of the National Health Service (Scotland) Act 1947 shall use their best endeavours to secure that, so far as practicable, in any hospital for which they are responsible a person who is suffering from a condition of chronic illness or disability and who –

(*a*) is in the hospital for the purpose of long-term care for that condition; or

(*b*) normally resides elsewhere but is being cared for in the hospital because –

(i) that condition is such as to preclude him from residing elsewhere without the assistance of some other person; and

(ii) such assistance is for the time being not available,

is not cared for in the hospital as an in-patient in any part of the hospital which is normally used wholly or mainly for the care of elderly persons, unless he is himself an elderly person.

(2) Each such Board as aforesaid shall provide the Secretary of State in such form and at such times as he may direct with such information as he may from time to time require as to any persons to whom subsection (1) of this section applied who, not being elderly persons, have been cared for in any hospital for which that Board are responsible in such a part of the hospital as is mentioned in that subsection; and the Secretary of State shall in each year lay before each House of Parliament such statement in such form as he considers appropriate of the information obtained by him under this subsection.

(3) In this section 'elderly person' means a person who is aged sixty-five or more or is suffering from the effects of premature ageing.

INFORMATION AS TO ACCOMMODATION OF YOUNGER WITH OLDER PERSONS UNDER PART III OF THE NATIONAL ASSISTANCE ACT 1948

18.–(1) The Secretary of State shall take steps to obtain from local authorities having functions under Part III of the National Assistance Act 1948 information as to the number of persons under the age of 65 appearing to the local authority in question to be persons to whom section 29 of that Act applies for whom residential accommodation is from time to time provided under section 21 (1)(*a*) or 26 (1)(*a*) of that Act at any premises in a part of those premises in which such accommodation is so provided for persons over that age.

(2) The Secretary of State shall take steps to obtain from local authorities having functions under the Social Work (Scotland) Act 1968 information as to the number of persons under the age of 65 who suffer from illness or mental disorder within the meaning of section 6 of the Mental Health (Scotland) Act 1960 or are substantially handicapped by any deformity or disability and for whom residential accommodation is from time to time provided under section 59 of the said Act of 1968 at any premises in a part of those premises in which such accommodation is so provided for persons over that age.

(3) Every local authority referred to in this section shall provide the

Secretary of State in such form and at such times as he may direct with such information as he may from time to time require for the purpose of this section; and the Secretary of State shall in each year lay before each House of Parliament such statement in such form as he considers appropriate of the information obtained by him under this section.

PROVISION OF INFORMATION RELATING TO CHIROPODY SERVICES

19. Every local health authority empowered to provide chiropody services under section 12 of the Health Services and Public Health Act 1968, or under section 27 of the National Health Service (Scotland) Act 1947, shall provide the Secretary of State in such form and at such times as he may direct with information as to the extent to which those services are available and used for the benefit of disabled persons under the age of sixty-five.

Miscellaneous provisions

USE OF INVALID CARRIAGES ON HIGHWAYS

20.–(1) In the case of a vehicle which is an invalid carriage complying with the prescribed requirements and which is being used in accordance with the prescribed conditions–

(*a*) no statutory provision prohibiting or restricting the use of footways shall prohibit or restrict the use of that vehicle on a footway;

(*b*) if the vehicle is mechanically propelled, it shall be treated for the purposes of the Road Traffic Act 1960, the Road Traffic Act 1962 the Road Traffic Regulation Act 1967 and Part I of the Road Safety Act 1967 as not being a motor vehicle; and

(*c*) whether or not the vehicle is mechanically propelled, it shall be exempted from the requirements of the Road Transport Lighting Act 1957.

(2) In this section–

'footway' means a way which is a footway, footpath or bridleway within the meaning of the Highways Act 1959; and in its application to Scotland means a way over which the public has a right of passage on foot only or a bridleway within the meaning of section 47 of the Countryside (Scotland) Act 1967;

'invalid carriage' means a vehicle, whether mechanically propelled or not, constructed or adapted for use for the carriage of one person, being a person suffering from some physical defect or disability;

'prescribed' means prescribed by regulations made by the Minister of Transport;

'statutory provision' means a provision contained in, or having effect under, any enactment.

(3) Any regulations made under this section shall be made by statu-

tory instrument, may make different provision for different circumstances and shall be subject to annulment in pursuance of a resolution of either House of Parliament.

BADGES FOR DISPLAY ON MOTOR VEHICLES USED BY DISABLED PERSONS

21.–(1) There shall be a badge of a prescribed form to be issued by local authorities for motor vehicles driven by, or used for the carriage of, disabled persons; and–

(*a*) subject to the provisions of this section, the badge so issued for any vehicle or vehicles may be displayed on it or on any of them either inside or outside the area of the issuing authority; and

(*b*) any power under section 84C of the Road Traffic Regulation Act 1967 (which was inserted by the Transport Act 1968) to make regulations requiring that orders under the Act shall include exemptions shall be taken to extend to requiring that an exemption given with reference to badges issued by one authority shall be given also with reference to badges issued by other authorities.

(2) A badge may be issued to a disabled person of any prescribed description resident in the area of the issuing authority for one or more vehicles which he drives and, if so issued, may be displayed on it or any of them at times where he is the driver.

(3) In such cases as may be prescribed, a badge may be issued to a disabled person of any prescribed description so resident for one or more vehicles used by him as a passenger and, if so issued, may be displayed on it or any of them at times when the vehicle is being used to carry him.

A badge may be issued to the same person both under this subsection and under subsection (2) above.

(4) A badge may be issued to an institution concerned with the care of the disabled for any motor vehicle or, as the case may be, for each motor vehicle kept in the area of the issuing authority and used by or on behalf of the institution to carry disabled persons of any prescribed description; and any badge so issued may be displayed on the vehicle for which it is issued at times when the vehicle is being so used.

(5) A local authority shall maintain a register showing the holders of badges issued by the authority under this section, and the vehicle or vehicles for which each of the badges is held; and in the case of badges issued to disabled persons the register shall show whether they were, for any motor vehicle, issued under subsection (2) or under subsection (3) or both.

(6) A badge issued under this section shall remain the property of the issuing authority, shall be issued for such period as may be prescribed, and shall be returned to the issuing authority in such circumstances as may be prescribed.

(7) Anything which is under this section to be prescribed shall be prescribed by regulations made by the Minister of Transport and Secretary of State by statutory instrument, which shall be subject to annulment in pursuance of a resolution of either House of Parliament; and regulations so made may make provision–

(*a*) as to the cases in which authorities may refuse to issue badges, and as to the fee (if any) which an authority may charge for the issue or re-issue of a badge; and

(*b*) as to the continuing validity or effect of badges issued before the coming into force of this section in pursuance of any scheme having effect under section 29 of the National Assistance Act 1948 or any similar scheme having effect in Scotland; and

(*c*) as to any transitional matters, and in particular the application to badges issued under this section of orders made before it comes into force and operating with reference to any such badges as are referred to in paragraph (*b*) above (being orders made, or having effect as if made, under the Road Traffic Regulation Act 1967).

(8) The local authorities for purposes of this section shall be the common council of the City of London, the council of a county or county borough in England or Wales or of a London borough and the council of a county or large burgh in Scotland; and in this section 'motor vehicle' has the same meaning as in the Road Traffic Regulation Act 1967.

(9) This section shall come into operation on such date as the Minister of Transport and Secretary of State may by order made by statutory instrument appoint.

ANNUAL REPORT ON RESEARCH AND DEVELOPMENT WORK

22. The Secretary of State shall as respects each year lay before Parliament a report on the progress made during that year in research and development work carried out by or on behalf of any Minister of the Crown in relation to equipment that might increase the range of activities and independence or well-being of disabled persons, and in particular such equipment that might improve the indoor and outdoor mobility of such persons.

WAR PENSIONS APPEALS

23.–(1) The Pensions Appeal Tribunals Act 1943 shall have effect with the amendments specified in the subsequent provisions of this section.

(2) In section 5–

(*a*) so much of subsection (1) as prevents the making of an appeal from an interim assessment of the degree of a disablement before the expiration of two years from the first notification of the making of an interim assessment (that is to say, the words from 'if' to 'subsection' where first occurring, and the words 'in force at the expiration of the said period of two years') is hereby repealed except in relation to a claim in the case of which the said first notification was given before the commencement of this Act;

(*b*) in the second paragraph of subsection (1) (which defines 'interim assessment' for the purposes of that subsection), for the words 'this subsection' there shall be substituted the words 'this section';

(*c*) in subsection (2) (which provides for an appeal to a tribunal from a Ministerial decision or assessment purporting to be a final settlement of a claim) at the end there shall be added the words 'and if the Tribunal so set aside the Minister's decision or assessment they may, if they think fit, make such interim assessment of the degree or nature of the disablement, to be in force until such date not later than two years after the making of the Tribunal's assessment, as they think proper';

(*d*) subsection (3) (which makes provision as to the coming into operation of section 5) is hereby repealed.

(3) In section 6, after subsection (2) there shall be inserted the following subsection–

'(2A) Where, in the case of such a claim as is referred to in section 1, 2, 3 or 4 of this Act–

(*a*) an appeal has been made under that section to the Tribunal and that appeal has been decided (whether with or without an appeal under subsection (2) of this section from the Tribunal's decision); but

(*b*) subsequently, on an application for the purpose made (in like manner as an application for leave to appeal under the said subsection (2)) jointly by the appellant and the Minister, it appears to the appropriate authority (that is to say, the person to whom under rules made under the Schedule to this Act any application for directions on any matter arising in connection with the appeal to the Tribunal fell to be made) to be proper so to do–

(i) by reason of the availability of additional evidence; or

(ii) (except where an appeal from the Tribunal's decision has been made under the said subsection (2)), on the ground of the Tribunal's decision being erroneous in point of law,

the appropriate authority may, if he thinks fit, direct that the decision on the appeal to the Tribunal be treated as set aside and the appeal from the Minister's decision be heard again by the Tribunal'.

(4) In subsection (3) of section 6 (under which, subject to subsection (2) of that section, a tribunal's decision is final and conclusive) for the words 'subject to the last foregoing subsection' there shall be substituted the words 'subject to subsections (2) and (2A) of this section'.

(5) In consequence of the Secretary of State for Social Services Order 1968, in section 12 (1), for the definition of 'the Minister' there shall be substituted the following:

' "the Minister" means the Secretary of State for Social Services'.

(6) This section extends to Northern Ireland.

INSTITUTE OF HEARING RESEARCH

24. The Secretary of State shall collate and present evidence to the Medical Research Council on the need for an institute for hearing research, such institute to have the general function of co-ordinating and promoting research on hearing and assistance to the deaf and hard of hearing.

SPECIAL EDUCATIONAL TREATMENT FOR THE DEAF-BLIND

25.–(1) It shall be the duty of every local education authority to provide the Secretary of State at such times as he may direct with information on the provision made by that local education authority of special educational facilities for children who suffer the dual handicap of blindness and deafness.

(2) The arrangements made by a local education authority for the special educational treatment of the deaf-blind shall, so far as is practicable, provide for the giving of such education in any school maintained or assisted by the local education authority.

(3) In the application of this section to Scotland for any reference to a local education authority there shall be substituted a reference to an educational authority within the meaning of section 145 of the Education (Scotland) Act 1962.

SPECIAL EDUCATIONAL TREATMENT FOR CHILDREN SUFFERING FROM AUTISM, etc.

26.–(1) It shall be the duty of every local education authority to provide the Secretary of State at such times as he may direct with information on the provision made by that local education authority of special educational facilities for children who suffer from autism or other forms of early childhood psychosis.

(2) The arrangements made by a local education authority for the special educational treatment of children suffering from autism and other forms of early childhood psychosis shall, so far as is practicable, provide for the giving of such education in any school maintained or assisted by the local education authority.

(3) In the application of this section to Scotland for any reference to a local education authority there shall be substituted a reference to an education authority within the meaning of section 145 of the Education (Scotland) Act 1962.

SPECIAL EDUCATIONAL TREATMENT FOR CHILDREN SUFFERING FROM ACUTE DYSLEXIA

27.–(1) It shall be the duty of every local education authority to provide the Secretary of State at such times as he may direct with information on the provision made by that local education authority of special educational facilities for children who suffer from acute dyslexia.

(2) The arrangements made by a local education authority for the special educational treatment of children suffering from acute dyslexia shall, so far as is practicable, provide for the giving of such education in any school maintained or assisted by the local education authority.

(3) In the application of this section to Scotland for any reference to a local education authority there shall be substituted a reference to an education authority within the meaning of section 145 of the Education (Scotland) Act 1962.

POWER TO DEFINE CERTAIN EXPRESSIONS

28. Where it appears to the Secretary of State to be necessary or expedient to do so for the proper operation of any provision of this Act, he may by regulations made by statutory instrument, which shall be subject to annulment in pursuance of a resolution of either House of Parliament, make provision as to the interpretation for the purposes of that provision of any of the following expressions appearing therein, that is to say, 'chronically sick', 'chronic illness', 'disabled' and 'disability'.

SHORT TITLE, EXTENT AND COMMENCEMENT

29.–(1) This Act may be cited as the Chronically Sick and Disabled Persons Act 1970.

(2) Sections 1 and 2 of this Act do not extend to Scotland.

(3) Save as otherwise expressly provided by sections 9, 14 and 23, this Act does not extend to Northern Ireland.

(4) This Act shall come into force as follows:–

(*a*) sections 1 and 21 shall come into force on the day appointed thereunder;

(*b*) sections 4, 5, 6, 7 and 8 shall come into force at the expiration of six months beginning with the date this Act is passed;

(*c*) the remainder shall come into force at the expiration of three months beginning with that date.

Document four
THE QUOTA SCHEME

The sections of the Disabled Persons (Employment) Act 1944 relating to the Quota Scheme are reprinted below.

DISABLED PERSONS (EMPLOYMENT) ACT 1944, SECTIONS 9–11

9.–(1) It shall be the duty of a person who has a substantial number of employees to give employment to persons registered as handicapped by disablement to the number that is his quota as ascertained in accordance with the next succeeding section, and, where he is not already doing so at times when vacancies occur, to allocate vacancies for that purpose; and the said duty shall be enforceable to the extent and in manner hereinafter in this section provided in the case of a person to whom this section applies, that is to say, a person who for the time being has, or in accordance with his normal practice and apart from transitory circumstances would have, in his employment persons to the number of not less than twenty (or such lower number as may be specified by an order made by the Minister for the time being in force).

Obligations as to employment of quota of registered persons in substantial staffs

(2) Subject to the provisions of the two next succeeding subsections, a person to whom this section applies shall not at any time take, or offer to take, into his employment any person other than a person registered as handicapped by disablement, if immediately after the taking in of that person the number of persons so registered in the employment of the person to whom this section applies (excluding persons employed by him in an employment of a class then designated under section twelve of this Act) would be less than his quota .

(3) Subsection (2) of this section shall not apply to a person's taking, or offering to take, into his employment at any time a person whom apart from that subsection it would have been his duty to take into his employment at that time either–

(*a*) by virtue of any Act, whether passed before or after the passing of this Act; or

(*b*) by virtue of an agreement to reinstate him in his employment entered into before the date appointed for the coming into operation of subsection (2) of this section.

(4) Subsection (2) of this section shall not apply to a person's taking, or offering to take, into his employment any person in accordance with a permit issued by the Minister under the subsequent provisions of this Act in that behalf.

(5) A person to whom this section applies who for the time being has in his employment a person registered as handicapped by disablement shall not, unless he has reasonable cause for doing so, discontinue the employment of that person, if immediately after the discontinuance the number of persons so registered in the employment of the person to whom this section applies (excluding persons employed by him in an employment of a class then designated under section twelve of this Act) would be less than his quota:

Provided that this subsection shall not have effect if immediately after the discontinuance the employer would no longer be a person to whom this section applies.

(6) Any person who contravenes subsection (2) or subsection (5) of this section shall be guilty of an offence and shall be liable on summary conviction to a fine not exceeding one hundred pounds or to imprisonment for a term not exceeding three months, or to both such fine and such imprisonment.

(7) A prosecution for a contravention of subsection (5) of this section shall not be instituted against any person unless–

(*a*) the matter has been referred to a district advisory committee;

(*b*) the committee, before considering the matter, has notified that person so as to give him an opportunity of making within a period not shorter than seven days from the sending or giving of the notification to him such representations to the committee as he may desire, either orally or in writing as he may desire; and

(*c*) the committee has made a report to the Minister.

On any such prosecution it shall not be necessary to prove compliance with the preceding provisions of this subsection unless the defendant so requires, and, if he so requires, a certificate purporting to be signed by or on behalf of the chairman of a district advisory committee that the matter in question has been referred to the committee under this subsection and that a notification and report has been made by them as therein provided shall be sufficient evidence of the facts stated therein until the contrary is shown.

Determination of employers' quotas.

10.–(1) The quota at any time of a person to whom section nine of this Act applies shall be a number ascertained in accordance with the provisions of this section.

(2) There shall be–

(*a*) a standard percentage; and

(*b*) a special percentage, either greater or smaller than the standard percentage, for employment in any trade or industry, or in any branch or part of any trade or industry, or for employment with any class of employer, being employment to which it appears to the Minister that a percentage other than the standard percentage ought to be assigned on the ground of its having distinctive characteristics as respects its suitability for disabled persons

(3) The standard percentage and any special percentage shall be such as may be specified by order made by the Minister, after consultation with such organisations representing employers and workers respectively, or both employers and workers, as he thinks fit, and an order assigning a special percentage shall contain such provisions as may appear to the Minister to be requisite for more particularly defining for the purposes of this section the trade or industry, branch or part of a trade or industry, or class of employer, to employment in which or with whom the percentage is assigned.

(4) The quota at any time of a person to whom section nine of this Act applies shall be the number ascertained by applying to the number of all the persons then in his employment (excluding persons employed by him in an employment of a class then designated under section twelve of this Act)–

(*a*) so far as they consist of persons employed by him in an employment other than one to which a special percentage is then assigned, the standard percentage; and

(*b*) so far as they consist of persons employed by him in an employment to which a special percentage is then assigned, that percentage:

Provided that if the number so ascertained includes or consists of a fraction less than one half the fraction shall be disregarded, and if the number so ascertained includes or consists of a fraction being one half or more the quota shall be the nearest higher whole number.

(5) On an application in that behalf made in the prescribed manner by any person to whom section nine of this Act applies representing that his quota, if ascertained in accordance with the last preceding subsection, or with that subsection together with any direction for the time being in force under this subsection, would be too great having regard to the particular circumstances in which all or any of the persons employed by him are employed, the Minister, if he is satisfied, after referring the application to a district advisory committee for their recommendations and considering their recommendations, that the representation is well founded, may direct that, during any such period ending not later than twelve months from the date of the direction as may be therein specified, the standard percentage, or any special percentage, or both, shall be reduced as specified in the direction for the purposes of the operation of the last preceding subsection in relation to the applicant.

(6) The Minister shall on an application in that behalf being made in the prescribed manner by any person to whom section nine of this Act applies and on his giving to the Minister all such information relevant to the application as he may require, determine what percentage of the number of all the persons in the employment of the applicant (excluding persons employed by him in an employment of a class for the time being designated under section twelve of this Act) his quota, as ascertained in accordance with the preceding provisions of this section, is likely to represent over any period ending not later than twelve months from the date of the determination, and shall furnish the applicant with a certificate stating that percentage and the period as respects which the determination was made, and the applicant shall be deemed to have in his employment at any time during the period stated in the certificate persons registered as handicapped by disablement to the number of his quota if the number of such persons then in his employment (excluding as aforesaid) reaches the percentage stated in the certificate of the number of all the persons then in his employment (excluding as aforesaid).

Permits for employment of persons not registered where quota condition not satisfied

11.–(1) On an application in that behalf being made in the prescribed manner by any person to whom section nine of this Act applies, the Minister may grant a permit for the purposes of subsection (4) of that section if it appears to him to be expedient so to do having regard to the nature of the work for which the applicant desires to take a person or persons into his employment and the qualifications and the suitability for the work of any persons or persons registered as handicapped by disablement who may be available therefor, or if he is satisfied that there is no such person or an insufficient number of such persons available therefor.

(2) A permit may be granted either unconditionally or subject to any conditions relating to the employment of the person or persons to whom the permit relates, and may be granted as respects the employment either of one or more persons specified or described therein or of a specified number of persons.

(3) If on an application being made as aforesaid the Minister is not satisfied that the case is one in which any permit, or such a permit as is applied for, ought to be granted, or is of opinion that conditions to which the applicant objects ought to be attached to a grant, then, if the applicant so requests, the Minister shall refer the application to a district advisory committee for their recommendations and shall determine what permit (if any) ought to be granted, and subject to what conditions (if any), only after considering the recommendations of the committee.

Document five
SHELTERED EMPLOYMENT

A document issued by the Department of Employment in 1973 reviewed the development of sheltered workshop provision for disabled people and summarized the views of the Tomlinson Report of 1941 which had recommended the establishment by central government of sheltered workshops – a recommendation which received statutory expression in section 15 of the Disabled Persons (Employment) Act 1944. Extracts from the review document are given below.

(2.6) It was the Tomlinson Committee, set up in 1941 to make recommendations on the employment needs of disabled people (including their rehabilitation) which first crystallised the concept of sheltered employment into a compound of welfare and real work with rehabilitation as the ideal. Their Report* condemned as 'wholly out of date' the notion that 'resettlement of the disabled must be a matter of philanthropy and good will'. While conceding that there would be a small group of severely disabled people who could not hold their own in open employment on level terms and under competitive conditions, and for whom provision should be made, the Committee felt that factors such as character and experience were more important than the disability itself in determining capacity; and they hoped that many people who at first appeared to be incapable of ordinary employment would be found able, after a period of specialised training and experience under sheltered conditions, to enter the ordinary employment field.

(2.24) Just as sheltered employment under the auspices of an employment department was in the Piercy Committee's view to be distinguished from diversionary or therapeutic or welfare arrangements so it was to be much more closely linked with ordinary employment, i.e. although sheltered, it should be on industrial lines, and as far as possible rehabilitative. Sheltered workshops should, according to the Piercy Report,† 'be

* Cmnd 6415, HMSO, London (1943).
† Cmnd 9883, HMSO, London (1957).

available only to those who are willing to undertake the work provided and able to make a significant contribution to production'; while those who were capable of only a 'modicum of effort and industry' should have separate arrangements made for them. The report also strongly insists that 'nothing could be worse than the prospect of a group of disabled people, some of them young on entering a workshop, remaining the whole of their working lives in a sheltered environment as a matter of course, and incidentally perhaps causing others with far better claims to sheltered work to be excluded'.

(3.51) But to find a place in Remploy, or any other sheltered workshop organized on industrial lines, for people who are not capable of the work could lead only to disappointment, and might, even if a permanent place could be found, lead to over-exertion and consequent health risks.

From: *Department of Employment, Sheltered Employment for Disabled People*, a consultative document issued by the Department of Employment, (1973).

Document six

THE ATTENDANCE ALLOWANCE

Social Security Act 1973.

ATTENDANCE ALLOWANCE

15.–(1) A person shall be entitled to an attendance allowance if he satisfies prescribed conditions as to residence or presence in Great Britain and either–

(*a*) he is so severely disabled physically or mentally that, by day, he requires from another person either–

(i) frequent attention throughout the day in connection with his bodily functions, or

(ii) continual supervision throughout the day in order to avoid substantial danger to himself or others; or

(*b*) he is so severely disabled physically or mentally that, at night, he requires from another person either–

(i) prolonged or repeated attention during the night in connection with his bodily functions, or

(ii) continual supervision throughout the night in order to avoid substantial danger to himself or others.

(2) Subject to the following provisions of this section, the period for which attendance allowance is payable to any person shall be that specified in a certificate issued in respect of him by the Attendance Allowance Board as being–

(*a*) a period throughout which he has satisfied or is likely to satisfy the condition mentioned in subsection (1) (*a*) above or that mentioned in (1) (*b*), or both; and

(*b*) a period immediately preceded by one of not less than 6 months throughout which he satisfied or is likely to satisfy one or both of those conditions;

and the weekly rate of the attendance allowance payable to a person for any period shall be the higher rate specified in relation thereto in Part I of Schedule 4 of this Act if the certificate states both as regards that period and as regards the preceding 6 months that he has satisfied or is likely to satisfy both those conditions, and shall be the lower rate so specified if the certificate does not so state.

(3) An attendance allowance shall not be payable to a person for any period preceding the date on which he makes a claim for it; but, except in so far as regulations otherwise provide–

(*a*) a claim for an attendance allowance may be made during the period of 6 months mentioned in subsection (2) (*b*) above, and an award may be made in pursuance of the claim subject to the condition that throughout that period the person to whom the claim relates satisfies the conditions there mentioned or, if the award is at the lower rate, one of those conditions; and

(*b*) an award so made may be reviewed if at any time it is found that during the period of the award or the interval between the making of the award and the beginning of that period the conditions so mentioned were at some time not both satisfied or, in the case of an award at the lower rate, were at some time not either of them satisfied.

(4) Regulations may provide that subsections (1) to (3) above, and any other provision of this Act so far as the provision relates to any of those subsections, shall have effect, in relation to any severely disabled person who is under the age of 16, subject to such modifications as may be prescribed; but nothing in this subsection authorises any increase in the rate of an attendance allowance.

(5) Regulations may provide that an attendance allowance shall not be payable in respect of a person for any period when he is a person for whom accommodation is provided–

(*a*) in pursuance of Part III of the National Assistance Act 1948, section 12 of the Health Services and Public Health Act 1968 or Part IV of the Social Work (Scotland) Act 1968; or

(*b*) in circumstances in which the cost is, or may be, borne wholly or partly out of public or local funds, in pursuance of any other enactment relating to persons under disability or to young persons or to education or training.

(6) The Attendance Allowance Board constituted under section 5 of the National Insurance Act 1970 shall continue in being by that name and have (in addition to the functions conferred on them by any provision of this Act other than this section)–

(*a*) the functions of advising the Secretary of State on such matters as he may refer to them relating to–

(i) the operation of the provisions of this Part of this Act in relation to attendance allowance (including questions as to the advisability of amending those provisions),

(ii) the exercise, in relation to attendance allowance, of his powers under those provisions; and

(*b*) such other functions, if any, as the Secretary of State may determine.

(7) Schedule 7 of this Act shall have effect with respect to the Attendance Allowance Board and their affairs; and–

(*a*) Part I to the Schedule relates to the Board's membership and the method by which their functions are to be performed;

(*b*) Part II relates to the Board's personnel, administration and expenses; and

(*c*) Part III relates to the Board's determination of questions arising in connection with claims and to reviews of determination and appeals therefrom;

but regulations may make further provision as to the constitution and procedure of the Board.

Document seven

THE MOBILITY ALLOWANCE

SOCIAL SECURITY PENSIONS ACT 1975.

22.–(1) In Chapter II of Part II of the principal Act (non-contributory benefits) the following is inserted after section 37–

37A.–(1) Subject to the provisions of this section, a person who satisfies prescribed conditions as to residence or presence in Great Britain shall be entitled to a mobility allowance for any period throughout which he is suffering from physical disablement such that he is either unable to walk or virtually unable to do so. Mobility allowance.

(2) Regulations may prescribe the circumstances in which a person is or is not to be treated for the purposes of this section as suffering from such physical disablement as is mentioned above; but a person qualifies for the allowance only if–

(*a*) his inability or virtual inability to walk is likely to persist for at least 12 months from the time when a claim for the allowance is received by the Secretary of State; and

(*b*) during most of that period his condition will be such as permits him from time to time to benefit from enhanced facilities for locomotion.

(3) The weekly rate of a mobility allowance shall be that specified in Schedule 4 to this Act, Part III, paragraph 3A.

(4) In the tax year 1976–77, and thereafter in each subsequent tax year, the Secretary of State shall consider whether the rate of mobility allowance should be increased having regard to the national economic situation as a whole, the general standard of living and such other matters as he thinks relevant.

(5) No person shall be entitled to a mobility allowance–

(*a*) in respect of a period in which he is under the age of 5 or over pensionable age;

(*b*) except in prescribed cases, for any week before that in which a claim for the allowance by or in respect of him is received by the Secretary of State.

(6) Regulations may prescribe cases in which mobility allowance is not

to be payable, or is to be payable at a reduced rate, while the person otherwise entitled has the use–

(*a*) of an invalid carriage or other vehicle provided by the Secretary of State under section 33 of the Health Services and Public Health Act 1968; or

(*b*) of any prescribed description of appliance supplied under the enactments relating to the National Health Service being such an appliance as is primarily designed to afford a means of personal and independent locomotion out of doors.

(7) Except so far as may be provided by regulations, the question of a person's entitlement to a mobility allowance shall be determined as at the date when a claim for the allowance is received by the Secretary of Sate.

(8) A payment to or in respect of any person by way of a mobility allowance, and the right to receive such a payment, shall (except in prescribed circumstances and for prescribed purposes) be disregarded in applying any enactment or instrument under which regard is to be had to a person's means.'

(2) In Part III of Schedule 4 to the principal Act there is inserted:

'3A. Mobility allowance . . . £5'.

(3) Regulations may make provision–

(*a*) for permitting a claim for a mobility allowance to be made, or treated as if made, for a period beginning after the date on which the claim is made;

(*b*) for permitting an award on any such claim to be made for a period beginning after the date on which the claim is made subject to the condition that the person in respect of whom the claim is made satisfies the prescribed requirements for entitlement when benefit becomes payable under the award;

(*c*) for the review of any such award if those requirements are found not to have been satisfied.

(4) Regulations may provide for disqualifying a person for receiving a mobility allowance for a period not exceeding six weeks on any disqualification if he fails without good cause to attend for, or to submit himself to, such medical or other examination or treatment as may be required in accordance with the regulations.

Document eight

THE INVALID CARE ALLOWANCE

INVALID CARE ALLOWANCE

7.–(1) Subject to the provisions of this section, a person shall be entitled to an invalid care allowance for any day on which he is engaged in caring for a severely disabled person if–

(*a*) he is regularly and substantially engaged in caring for that person; and

(*b*) he is not gainfully employed; and

(*c*) the severely disabled person is either such relative of his as may be prescribed or a person of any such other description as may be prescribed.

(2) A person shall not be entitled to an allowance under this section if he is under the age of sixteen or receiving full-time education; and a woman shall not be entitled to any such allowance if–

(*a*) she is married and either–

(i) she is residing with her husband; or

(ii) he is contributing to her maintenance at a weekly rate of such an allowance; or

(*b*) she is cohabiting with a man as his wife.

(3) A person shall not be entitled to an allowance under this section unless he satisfies prescribed conditions as to residence or presence in Great Britain.

(4) A person who has attained pensionable age shall not be entitled to an allowance under this section unless he was entitled (or is treated by regulations as having been entitled) to such an allowance immediately before attaining that age; and regulations may make provision whereby a person who has attained retiring age and was entitled to such an allowance immediately before attaining that age continues to be entitled to such an allowance notwithstanding that he is not caring for a severely disabled person or no longer satisfies the requirements of subsection (1) (*a*) or (*b*) above.

(5) No person shall be entitled for the same day to more than one allowance under this section; and where, apart from this subsection, two or more persons would be entitled for the same day to such an allowance in

respect of the same severely disabled person, one of them only shall be entitled, being such one of them as they may jointly elect in the prescribed manner or as may, in default of such election, be determined by the Secretary of State in his discretion.

(6) Regulations may prescribe the circumstances in which a person is or is not to be treated for the purposes of this section as engaged, or regularly and substantially engaged, in caring for a severely disabled person, as gainfully employed or as receiving full-time education.

(7) An allowance under this section shall be payable at the weekly rate specified in relation thereto in Part I of Schedule 4 to the Social Security Act 1973; and that rate shall, in such circumstances as may be prescribed, be increased for child or adult dependants by the appropriate amount specified in relation thereto in Part III of that Schedule.

(8) In this section–

'severely disabled person' means a person in respect of whom there is payable either an attendance allowance or such other payment out of public funds on account of his need for attendance as may be prescribed;

'relative' includes a person who is a relative by marriage or adoption and a person who would be a relative if some person born illegitimate had been born legitimate;

'retiring age' has the same meaning as in section 6 above.

(9) Any question which under subsection (5) above falls to be determined by the Secretary of State in his discretion shall be included among the questions to which subsection (1) of section 84 of the said Act of 1973 applies; and in subsection (3) of that section, section 66 (2) of the National Insurance Act 1965 and section 65 (2) of the National Insurance Act (Northern Ireland) 1966 references to questions within section 84 (1) (*d*) shall include references to any such question as aforesaid.

From Social Security Benefits Act 1975, section 7.

Document nine
ENTITLEMENT TO MOBILITY ALLOWANCE

In 1979 the Regulations specifying the circumstances which would qualify an individual to receive the mobility allowance were changed. The revised wording encompassed individuals unable to walk due to severe behaviour disorders caused by mental handicap resulting from organic conditions.

(3)(1) A person shall only be treated, for the purposes of Section 37A, as suffering from physical disablement such that he is either unable to walk or virtually unable to do so, if his physical condition as a whole is such that, without having regard to circumstances peculiar to that person as to place of residence or as to place of, or nature of, employment–

(*a*) he is unable to walk: or
(*b*) his ability to walk out of doors is so limited, as regards the distance over which or the speed at which or the length of time for which or the manner in which he can make progress on foot without severe discomfort, that he is virtually unable to walk: or
(*c*) the exertion required to walk would constitute a danger to his life or would be likely to lead to a serious deterioration in his health.

(2) A person shall not be treated, for the purposes of section 37A as suffering from physical disablement such that he is either unable to walk or virtually unable to do so if he is not unable or virtually unable to walk with a prosthesis or an artificial aid which he habitually wears or uses or if he would not be unable or virtually unable if he habitually wore or used a prosthesis or an artificial aid which is suitable in his case.

From: Mobility Allowance Regulations 1975 (Section 37A) as amended by Statutory Instrument 1979/72.

Document ten
THE NON-CONTRIBUTORY INVALIDITY PENSION

NON-CONTRIBUTORY INVALIDITY PENSION

6.–(1) Subject to the provisions of this section, a person shall be entitled to a non-contributory invalidity pension for any day on which he is incapable of work if he has been incapable of work for a period of not less than one hundred and ninety-six consecutive days ending immediately before that day.

(2) A person shall not be entitled to any such pension if he is under the age of sixteen or receiving full-time education; and a woman shall not be entitled to any such pension if–

(*a*) she is married and either–

(i) she is residing with her husband; or

(ii) he is contributing to her maintenance at a weekly rate not less than the weekly rate of such a pension; or

(*b*) she is cohabiting with a man as his wife,

except where she is incapable of performing normal household duties.

(3) A person shall not be entitled to any such pension unless he satisfies prescribed conditions as to residence or presence in Great Britain.

(4) A person who has attained pensionable age shall not be entitled to a pension under this section unless he was entitled (or is treated by regulations as having been entitled) to such a pension immediately before attaining that age; and regulations may make provision whereby a person who has attained retiring age and was entitled to such a pension immediately before attaining that age continues to be entitled to such a pension notwithstanding that he is not incapable of work or no longer satisfies the requirements of subsection (1) above as to the period for which a person must have been incapable of work.

(5) Regulations may make provision whereby, in the case of a person who has previously been entitled to a pension under this section, the requirement of subsection (1) above as to the period for which a person must have been incapable of work may be satisfied by reference to a period not ending immediately before the day there mentioned or not consisting of consecutive days.

(6) Regulations may prescribe the circumstances in which a person is or is not to be treated for the purposes of this section as incapable of work, as incapable of performing normal household duties or as receiving full-time education.

(7) A pension under this section shall be payable at the weekly rate specified in relation thereto in Part I of Schedule 4 to the Social Security Act 1973; and that rate shall, in circumstances as may be prescribed, be increased for child or adult dependants by the appropriate amount specified in relation thereto in Part III of that Schedule.

From: Social Security Benefits Act 1975, section 6.

Document eleven
MAKING IT HARDER FOR HOUSEWIVES

Less than a year after the introduction of the housewife's non-contributory invalidity pension, the Regulations governing eligibility were amended to impose stiffer qualifying conditions, as may be seen by comparing the original wording of Regulation 13A below with the revised version which is given beneath.

13A Circumstances in which a woman is or is not to be treated as incapable of performing normal household duties.

(1) A woman shall not be treated as incapable of performing normal household duties unless she is so incapable by reason of some specific disease or bodily or mental disablement.

(2) Where as a result of such disease or disablement a woman–

(*a*) is unable to perform to any substantial extent, or cannot reasonably be expected to perform to any substantial extent, normal household duties: or

(*b*) in the absence of substantial assistance from or supervision by another person, is unable to perform to any substantial extent, or cannot reasonably be expected to perform to any substantial extent, such duties

she may be treated as incapable of performing such duties.

AMENDMENT OF REGULATION 13A OF THE PRINCIPAL REGULATIONS

In regulation 13A of the principal regulations (circumstances in which a woman is or is not to be treated as incapable of performing normal household duties) for paragraph (2) there shall be substituted the following paragraph:

(2) A woman shall be treated as incapable of performing normal household duties if, without substantial assistance from or supervision by another person, she cannot or cannot reasonably be expected to perform such duties to any substantial extent, but she shall not be treated as so incapable if, without such assistance or supervision, she can or can reasonably be expected to perform such duties to any substantial extent.

From: Non-contributory Invalidity Pension Regulations (Statutory Instrument 1977/1312 Section 13A and Amendment Regulation Statutory Instrument 1978/1340).

Document twelve

RESIDENTIAL CARE AND LOCAL AUTHORITY RESPONSIBILITIES

PROVISION OF ACCOMMODATION

(2)(1) It shall be the duty of every local authority, subject to and in accordance with the provisions of this part of this Act, to provide–

(*a*) residential accommodation for persons who by reason of age, infirmity or any other circumstances are in need of care and attention which is not otherwise available to them:

(*b*) temporary accommodation for persons who are in urgent need thereof, being need arising in circumstances which could not reasonably have been foreseen or in such other circumstances as the authority may in any particular case determine.

(2) In the exercise of their said duty a local authority shall have regard to the welfare of all persons for whom accommodation is provided, and in particular to the need for providing accommodation of different descriptions suited to different descriptions of such persons as are mentioned in the last foregoing subsection.

(3) A local authority shall exercise their functions under this section in accordance with a scheme made thereunder.

(4) Accommodation provided by a local authority in the exercise of their said functions shall be provided in premises managed by the authority, or, to such extent as may be specified in the scheme under this section, in such premises managed by another local authority as may be agreed between the two authorities and on such terms, including terms as to the reimbursement of expenditure incurred by the said other authority, as may be so agreed.

26(1) Notwithstanding anything in the foregoing provisions of this part of this Act, a scheme under section twenty-one thereof may provide for the making by a local authority, in lieu or in supplementation of the provision of accommodation in premises managed by them or another local authority, of arrangements with a voluntary organization managing any premises for the provision of accommodation in those premises.

(2) Any such arrangements as aforesaid shall provide for the making by the local authority to the organization of payments in respect of the accommodation provided at such rates as may be determined by or under the arrangements.

From: National Assistance Act 1948.

TABLE OF STATUTES

1893 Elementary Education (Blind and Deaf Children) Act
1899 Elementary Education (Defective and Epileptic Children) Act
1911 National Insurance Act
1918 Education Act
1919 Disabled Men (Facilities for Employment) Act
1920 Blind Persons Act
1944 Disabled Persons (Employment) Act
1944 Education Act
1946 National Health Service Act
1948 National Assistance Act
1958 Disabled Persons (Employment) Act
1959 Mental Health Act
1970 National Insurance (Old persons' and widows' pensions and attendance allowance) Act
1970 Chronically Sick and Disabled Persons Act
1970 Education (Handicapped Children) Act
1971 National Insurance Act
1973 Social Security Act
1975 Social Security Pensions Act
1975 Social Security Benefits Act
1976 Education Act
1978 Rating (Disabled Persons) Act
1980 Housing Act
1980 Social Security Act
1980 Social Security (No. 2) Act

TABLE OF RELEVANT OFFICIAL REPORTS

1889 Report of the Royal Commission on the Blind, the Deaf and Dumb, etc., of the United Kingdom, C 5781, Vol. xix.
1898 Report of a Departmental Committee on Defective and Epileptic Children, C 8746, Vol. xxvi.
1943 Report of the Inter-Departmental Committee on the Rehabilitation and Resettlement of Disabled Persons, Cmnd 6415, HMSO.
1957 Report of the Committee of Inquiry on the Rehabilitation, Training and Resettlement of Disabled Persons, Cmnd 9883, Vol. xiv.
1957 Royal Commission on the Law Relating to Mental Illness and Mental Deficiency, Cmnd 169, HMSO.
1968 Report of the Committee on Local Authority and Allied Personal Social Services, Cmnd 3703, HMSO.
1969 Report of an Advisory Committee on the Health and Welfare of Handicapped Persons, *People with Epilepsy*, HMSO.
1971 Department of Employment, *Services for the Disabled*, HMSO.
1971 Office of Population Censuses and Surveys, *Handicapped and Impaired in Great Britain*, HMSO.
1971 Report of a Home Office Working Party, *Habitual Drunken Offenders*, HMSO.
1971 Department of Health and Social Security, *Better Services for the Mentally Handicapped*, Cmnd 4683, HMSO.
1972 Report of a Sub-Committee of the Standing Medical Advisory Committee, *Rehabilitation*, HMSO.
1972 Report of the Committee of Enquiry into the Education of the Visually Handicapped, HMSO.

1972 Department of Employment discussion document, *Resettlement Policy and Services for Disabled People.*
1973 Department of Employment discussion document, *Quota Scheme for Disabled People.*
1973 Department of Employment discussion document, *Sheltered Employment for Disabled People.*
1974 Department of Health and Social Security, *Mobility of Physically Disabled People*, HMSO.
1975 Department of Health and Social Security, *Better Services for the Mentally Ill*, Cmnd 6233, HMSO.
1976 Department of Health and Social Security, *Priorities for Health and Personal Social Services*, HMSO.
1976 Report of the Committee on Child Health Services, Cmnd 6684, HMSO.
1976 Department of Health and Social Security report of the Working Party on Manpower Training for the Social Services.
1976 Department of Health and Social Security, *Review of the Mental Health Act 1959*, HMSO.
1978 Report of the Royal Commission on Civil Liability and Compensation for Personal Injury, Cmnd 7054, HMSO.
1978 Report of the Committee of Inquiry into the Education of Handicapped Children and Young People, Cmnd 7212, HMSO.
1979 Report of the Committee of Enquiry into Mental Handicap Nursing and Care, Cmnd 7468, HMSO.
1979 Manpower Services Commission discussion document, *Sheltered Employment for Disabled People.*
1980 Department of Education and Science, *Special Needs in Education*, Cmnd 7996, HMSO.
1980 Department of Health and Social Services report on Inequalities in Health.

TABLE OF RELEVANT NON-OFFICIAL REPORTS

1964 United Nations Department of Social and Economic Affairs, *Study on the Legislative and Administrative Aspects of Rehabilitation of the Disabled in Selected Countries*.

1973 Economist Intelligence Unit report, *Care With Dignity*, National Fund for Research into Crippling Diseases, Sussex.

1974 Disablement Income Group report, *Realizing a National Disability Income*.

1976 Snowdon Working Party Report, *Integrating the Disabled*, National Fund for Research into Crippling Diseases, Sussex.

1977 Personal Social Services Council, *Residential Care Reviewed*.

1978 Economist Intelligence Unit study of the welfare benefit system as it affects disabled people, *Whose Benefit*?

1979 Silver Jubilee Committee Report on Improving Access for Disabled People, *Can Disabled People Go Where You Go*?, DHSS.

SELECT BIBLIOGRAPHY

ANDERSON, E. M., *The Disabled Schoolchild*, Methuen, London (1973).

BARANYAY, E., *A Lifetime of Learning*, National Society for Mentally Handicapped Children, London (1976).

BAYLEY, M., *Mental Handicap and Community Care*, Routledge & Kegan Paul, London (1973).

BLAXTER, M., *The Meaning of Disability*, Heinemann, London (1976).

BONDO, U., *Ida: Life with my Handicapped Child*, Faber & Faber, London (1980).

BOSWELL, D.M. AND WINGROVE, J. M. (eds), *The Handicapped Person in the Community*, Tavistock Publications, London (1974).

BREARLEY, P., GIBBONS, J., MILES, A., TOPLISS, E., AND WOODS, G., *The Social Context of Health Care*, Basil Blackwell & Martin Robertson, Oxford (1978).

BRITISH COUNCIL FOR REHABILITATION OF THE DISABLED, *The Handicapped School Leaver*, BCRD, London (1964).

BUCHANAN, J. M., AND CHAMBERLAIN, M A., *Survey of the Mobility of the Disabled in an Urban Environment*, Royal Association of Disability and Rehabilitation, London (1978).

BUCKLEY, J. R., *Work and Housing of Impaired Persons in Great Britain*, HMSO, London (1971).

BURTON, L., *The Family Life of Sick Children*, Routledge & Kegan Paul, London (1975).

CAMPLING, J., *Better Lives for Disabled Women*, Virago Press, London (1979).

CAMPLING, J., (ed.), *Images of Ourselves*, Routledge & Kegan Paul, London (1981).

CENTRAL OFFICE OF INFORMATION, *Care of Disabled People in Britain*, HMSO, London (1975).

CLARKE, A. M. AND CLARKE, A. D. B. (eds), *Mental Deficiency : the Changing Outlook* (3rd edn.), Methuen, London (1974).

CRAFT, M. AND CRAFT, A., *Sex and the Mentally Handicapped*, Routledge & Kegan Paul, London (1978).

DHSS, *Census of Mentally Handicapped Patients in England and Wales at the end of 1970*, HMSO, London (1972).

DHSS, *Census of Residential Accommodation 1970*, HMSO, London (1976).

DISABILITY ALLIANCE, *Disability Rights Handbook*, Disability Alliance, London, (published annually).

ELLIOTT, J. AND WHELAN, E. (eds), *Employment of Mentally Handicapped People*, King's Fund Paper No. 8, King's Fund, London (1975).

FORSYTHE, E., *Living with Multiple Sclerosis*, Faber & Faber, London (1979).

GOFFMAN, E., *Asylums*, Doubleday, New York (1961).

GOFFMAN, E., *Stigma*, Prentice Hall, New Jersey (1963).

GOLDSMITH, S., 'Mobility Housing', *Conference Proceedings of the 2nd European Conference of Rehabilitation International*, NAIDEX Kent (1978).

GREENGROSS, W., *Entitled to Love*, National Marriage Guidance Council, London (1976).

HANNAM, C., *Parents and Mentally Handicapped Children*, Penguin, Harmondsworth (1975).

HARRIS, A. I., *Handicapped and Impaired in Great Britain*, HMSO, London (1971).

HARRIS, A. I., SMITH, C.R.W., AND HEAD, E., *Income and Entitlement to Supplementary Benefit of Impaired People in Great Britain*, HMSO, London (1972).

HEWETT, S., *The Family and the Handicapped Child*, George Allen & Unwin, London (1970).

HUNT, P. (ed.), *Stigma*, Geoffrey Chapman, London (1966).

HYMAN, M., *The Extra Costs of Disabled Living*, National Fund for Research into Crippling Diseases, Sussex (1977).

JONES, K., *A History of the Mental Health Services*, Routledge & Kegan Paul, London (1972).

JONES, K., *Opening the Door*, Routledge & Kegan Paul, London (1975).

KEEBLE, U., *Aids and Adaptations*, Bedford Square Press, London (1979).

KEW, S., *Handicap and Family Crisis*, Pitmans, London (1975).

KING, R. D., RAYNES, N. V., AND TIZARD, J., *Patterns of Residential Care*, Routledge & Kegan Paul, London (1971).

LANCASTER-GAYE, D., *Personal Relationships, the Handicapped and the Community*, Routledge & Kegan Paul, London (1972).

LEES, D., AND SHAW, S. (eds), *Impairment, Disability and Handicap*, Social Science Research Council, Heinemann, London (1974).

McCORMACK, M., *A Mentally Handicapped Child in the Family*, Constable, London (1979).

McMICHAEL, J., *A Study of Physically Handicapped Children and their Families*, Staples Press, London (1971).

MATTINSON, J., *Marriage and Mental Handicap*, Duckworth, London (1970).

MILLER, E. J. AND GWYNNE, G. V., *A Life Apart*, Tavistock, London (1972).

MITTLER, P. (ed.), *The Psychological Assessment of Mental and Physical Handicaps*, Methuen, London (1970).

MITTLER, P., *People not Patients*, Methuen, London (1978).

MORRIS, A., *No Feet to Drag*, Sidgwick & Jackson, London (1972).

MORRIS, P., *Put Away*, Routledge & Kegan Paul, London (1969).

OFFICE OF HEALTH ECONOMICS, *Mental Handicap: Ways Forward*, OHE, London (1978).

OSWIN, M., *The Empty Hours*, Penguin Books, Harmondsworth (1973).

OSWIN, M., *Children Living in Long-Stay Hospitals*, Spastics International Medical Publications, London (1978).

OSWIN, M., *Holes in the Welfare Net*, Bedford Square Press, London (1978).

PRITCHARD, D. G., *Education and the Handicapped*, Routledge & Kegan Paul, London (1963).

PUGH, G., AND RUSSELL, P., *Shared Care : Support Services for Families with Mentally Handicapped Children*, National Children's Bureau, London (1977).

ROBINSON, T., *In Worlds Apart*, Bedford Square Press, London (1978).

RUTTER, M., TIZARD, J., AND WHITMORE, K. (eds), *Education, Health and Behaviour*, Longmans, London (1970).

SAINSBURY, S., *Registered as Disabled*, Occasional Papers in Social Administration No. 35, Bell, London (1970).

SAINSBURY, S., *Measuring Disability*, Occasional Papers in Social Administration No. 54, Bell, London (1973).

SPAIN, B., AND WIGLEY, G. (eds), *Right from the Start : a Service for Preschool Handicapped Children*, National Society for Mentally Handicapped Children, London (1975).

STEVENS, M., *The Educational and Social Needs of Children with Severe Handicap* (Second Edition), Edward Arnold, London (1976).

STEVENS, M., *Observe – Then Teach* (2nd. edn.), Edward Arnold, London (1978).

STEWART, W. F. R., *Sex and the Physically Handicapped*, National Fund for Research into Crippling Diseases, Sussex (1976).

STEWART, W. F. R., *The Sexual Side of Handicap*, Woodhead – Faulkener, Cambridge (1979).

STONE, J. AND TAYLOR, F., *Handbook for Parents with a Handicapped Child*, Arrow Books, London (1977).

TESTER, S., *Housing Services for Disabled People*, Housing Development Directorate Occasional Paper No. 3/78, Department of the Environment, London (1978).

THOMAS, D., *The Social Psychology of Childhood Disability*, Methuen, London (1978).

THOMAS, D., FIRTH, H. AND KENDALL, A., *ENCOR – A Way Ahead*, Campaign for the Mentally Handicapped, London (1978).

TIZARD, J. AND GRAD, J. C., *The Mentally Handicapped and their Families*, Oxford University Press (1961).

TOPLISS, E., *Provision for the Disabled* (2nd. edn.), Basil Blackwell & Martin Robertson, Oxford (1979).

TOPLISS E. AND GOULD, B., *Charter for the Disabled*, Basil Blackwell & Martin Robertson, Oxford (1981).

TUCKEY, L., PARFITT, J. AND TUCKEY, B., *Handicapped School Leavers*, National Children's Bureau, London (1973).

TYNE, A., *Residential Provision for Adults who are Mentally Handicapped*, Campaign for the Mentally Handicapped, London (1977).

TYNE A., *Looking at Life in a Hospital, Hostel, Home or Unit*, Campaign for the Mentally Handicapped, London (1978).

VOYSEY, M., *A Constant Burden*, Routledge & Kegan Paul, London (1975).

WHELAN, E. AND SPEAKE, B., *Adult Training Centres in England and Wales*, Hester Adrian Research Centre, University of Manchester (1977).

WRIGHT, B, *Physical Disability – a Psychological Approach*, Harper, New York (1960).

WYNN, M. AND WYNN, A., *Prevention of Handicap of Perinatal Origin*, Foundation for Education and Research in Childbearing, London (1976).

YOUNGHUSBAND, E., BIRCHALL, D., DAVIE, R., AND KELLMER-PRINGLE, M., *Living with Handicap*, National Bureau for Co-operation in Child Care, London (1970).

INDEX